What People Are Saying About Donna Kunde and Dr. James Bryant

Many of the voices you'll hear in these pages have also been part of the Podcast Profit Mastermind. Their testimonials reflect not only their results but also their experience walking this journey together.

"Monetizing a podcast can feel like an uphill struggle, especially when you don't know what you don't know. After going it alone for four years, joining the weekly Podcast Profit Mastermind has been a wake-up call. I realized I had a podcast, but not a system. Donna Kunde and James Bryant know how to turn a podcast into a sustainable, profitable business by asking the right questions and guiding us toward actionable answers. I'm constantly inspired by the business acumen and generosity in this group as challenges—big and small—are discussed and solved in such a supportive space."
— *Mariette Snyman, Host of Calm, Clear & Helpful Podcast*

"James is exceptional at helping me make sense of the chaos. He helped me focus my energy, strengthen my mindset, and celebrate who I am beyond my achievements. His engineering and investment background makes me feel understood, and the accountability he's built through his community has kept me aligned with both my life and wealth goals. Coaching with James has been invaluable."
— *Tiffany M. Ward, IT Professional & Real Estate Investor*

"Donna brings warmth, clarity, and confidence to everything she teaches. Her down-to-earth approach connects with people in a genuine way, inspiring them to believe in their ability to create change. I've had the pleasure of learning from her more than once, and each time I walk away encouraged and ready to take action."
— *Lee Cooper, Assistant Branch Manager*

"Even when I'm not the one in the hot seat, I get a lot out of every session. Listening to what others are working through always sparks new ideas for me. Sometimes the mastermind feels like drinking from a firehose, but all it takes is one drop of insight to change everything. That's what I love about this group. The knowledge that gets shared each week keeps me thinking, improving, and moving forward."

— Kevin L. Beers, Co-Host, Survival Mode Podcast

"Donna provided a professionally polished program which enabled high levels of participation. She provided a practical and highly DOABLE process to initiate desirable change and set goals. Thank you, Donna!"

— Jim Hasbrouck, Innkeeper

"From our very first session, James created a safe space for me to be honest about my goals and challenges. His deep listening, thoughtful questions, and practical feedback helped me see new possibilities and approach my work differently. He balances compassion with challenge in a way that pushes you to grow. James is an outstanding executive coach, and I highly recommend him."

— Taiwo Ajayi, Senior Program Manager,
AI & Cloud Transformation

Interacting with Donna and James is a pleasure. They complement each other to create the perfect environment for learning. They always leave me motivated to achieve more and with a sense of "you can do this".

— Jeremy Gray, Three Continents Consulting

"As a leader working 60-hour weeks, I felt like my business was running my life. Coaching with James changed everything. I now work less, earn more, and—most importantly—am fully present with my family instead of just saying they're a priority. It's easy to lose sight of who we're doing all of this for. James helped me reclaim that clarity and build a life that supports what matters most."

— Jerome Myers, P.E., Meyers Development Group

"*The time I invest each week with my fellow radio show hosts pays off immediate benefits. Every one of them is an expert in their field. And every one of us is wrestling with similar challenges: being heard, and seen. Being easy to follow, easy to work with, and easy to get paid. Every week we share our successes and challenges and every week we grow. Together, we are stronger and Donna and James have created a fertile environment for our success.*"

— *Gayle Turner, The Storytellers Channel*

"*James helped me shift from saying 'this went well, but…' to 'this went well, and…,' which allowed me to fully acknowledge my achievements instead of diminishing them. His coaching sharpened my focus, clarified my goals, and made my time more productive and fulfilling. That simple shift changed how I lead and how I show up in my work.*"

— *Wilf Nixon, Professional Snow Fighters Association*

Influencers Formula® Presents

YOUR MESSAGE IS THE BUSINESS

HOW EVERYDAY CREATORS BUILD INFLUENCE, IMPACT, AND INCOME THROUGH PODCASTING

DONNA KUNDE | DR. JAMES BRYANT
SHEILA SLICK | CHRIS O'BYRNE |
GAYLE TURNER | SHELLI JOST BRADY
KEVIN L. BEERS | WAYNE CARROLL |
MARIETTE SNYMAN | RAJ KAPUR
BERTRAM G. ROBINSON SR. |
MICHAEL A. GRANT JR.

This book was developed from podcast conversations transcribed using PodToBook.ai. All content has been reviewed, verified, edited, and refined by the author prior to publication.

ISBN: 979-8-89079-438-3 (ebook)
ISBN: 979-8-89079-434-5 (paperback)
ISBN: 979-8-89079-435-2 (hardback)

Leadership Awake Press

Published by FeelGD, LLC

First Edition, 2025

For more information and resources, visit www.podcastprofitsystem.com

DISCLAIMER

The information provided in this book is for educational and informational purposes only. It does not constitute professional advice and should not be used as a substitute for consultation with professional advisors.

While the author has made every effort to provide accurate information and helpful strategies, individual results may vary. The practices and systems described in this book are based on the author's personal experience and observations.

The author and publisher make no guarantees concerning the level of success you may experience by following the advice and strategies contained in this book. Results will differ for each individual based on their background, dedication, business savvy, and countless other factors.

Any examples, stories, or case studies included are not intended to represent or guarantee that anyone will achieve the same or similar results. Each person's success depends on their unique circumstances, effort, and abilities.

By reading this book, you assume all risks associated with using the advice given, with full understanding that you, solely, are responsible for anything that may occur as a result of putting this information into action, regardless of your interpretation of the advice.

Dedication

To all those making a difference behind the mic—this is for you.

May these pages bring you the encouragement and guidance you've been searching for to keep going, keep creating, and keep sharing your voice with the world.

Your message matters more than you know.

TABLE OF CONTENTS

PART III
INFLUENCE IN ACTION

Section A – Understanding Influence

Section B – Expressing Influence

PART IV
MONETIZATION SYSTEMS

PART V
FUTURE-PROOF YOUR INFLUENCE

FOREWORD

If you're reading this book, chances are you've got (or want) a podcast, you've got a message that you've got to share, and you're wondering, "Is all this work actually attracting clients and creating real impact?

That's a critical question.
Good job for asking.

I've spent years helping purpose-driven consultants, coaches, and small business owners turn their ideas into high-quality, client-attracting, impact-making books.

If you're doing a podcast, I imagine you'll want the same: high-quality, client-attracting, impact-making content.

Good job for reading this book.

You'll discover how to turn past episodes into real business assets, give your listeners an easy and natural next step with you, and align your podcast with offers that actually pay you.

Donna brings years of experience helping creators publish thousands of episodes and reach over a million downloads, not as a fame game, but as a courage-and-service game. James brings clarity, structure, and the business brain that turns all that heart into sustainable revenue.

Together, they've built a calm, ethical, and practical way to turn your podcast from "nice content" into an on-ramp for the work you're really here to do.

Along the way, you'll learn how to be seen by the right people, be heard in a way that makes listeners feel truly known, be easy to follow with clear and simple next steps, be the solution with offers that match real problems, and be paid with purpose in a way that feels honest and aligned.

No more hoping it "somehow" turns into business.

If you let it, this book will gently rewire how you think about your show. You'll start to see your podcast as a doorway into your business, not the whole house. You'll realize you already have enough content; you just need better pathways.

You'll measure success by connections, clients, and change, not just stats. And you'll make invitations that feel natural, warm, and human. Most of all, you'll stop waiting to be "big enough" or "ready enough."

Your message is an asset. Your podcast can be a business. And the people who need you?

They're already listening.

This book will help them find their way to your door.

Enjoy!

Cheers,

Ben

— Ben Gioia, Book Writing Coach and Publisher, Influence With A Heart® and Leadership Awake Press

OUR WARMEST WELCOME TO YOU

Hi, it's Donna and James,

You started your podcast because you have something meaningful to share. A message, a story, or a mission that matters. At some point, every podcaster begins to wonder the same thing we did:

How do you turn that message into a business that grows your income, expands your influence, and creates lasting impact without spending every waking hour creating new content or chasing sponsors?

Ralph Waldo Emerson once wrote, "The creation of a thousand forests is in one acorn." We believe your message is that acorn. Inside it is the potential to grow into something much greater—a body of work that continues to serve others while supporting the life and business you're building.

That belief is the heart of *Your Message Is the Business* and the system behind it, the Podcast Profit System™. Together, they offer a simple, practical way to turn your podcast into a sustainable business that truly works for you.

You don't need a massive audience or a big marketing budget to succeed. What you need is structure, clarity, and a system that helps you turn your ideas into assets. That's what this book will help you build.

Here, you'll learn how to earn from your message by using what you already have. You'll find a process that keeps you organized and moving forward. You'll also find tools, coaching insights, and amplified-intelligence prompts that give you the confidence to take the next step.

This book walks you through the same process we use with our clients to move from content creation to consistent monetization in as little as ninety days.

Thank you for trusting us to walk beside you. We're honored to help you build, grow, and strengthen your influence through the power of your voice and your message.

With gratitude,
Donna & James

ACCESS YOUR BOOK BONUSES

SCAN ME

SCAN THE CODE TO GET YOUR RESOURCES, WORKSHEETS, AND NEXT STEPS.

PART I

WHY THIS BOOK, WHY NOW

If you are a coach, consultant, author, or creator who wants your podcast to do more than share ideas, this section is your starting point. You will see how your lived experience, your message, and your listener's needs come together to build real connection. By the end of Part I, you'll understand why influence begins with clarity, trust, and a voice your audience can follow.

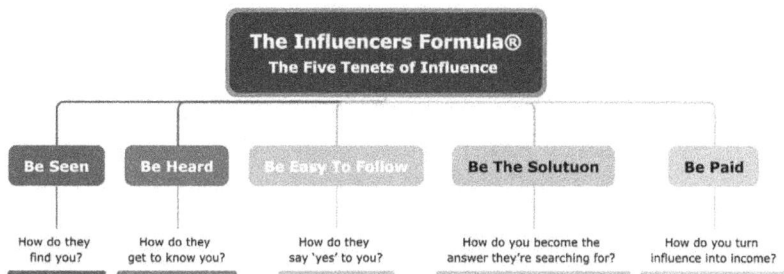

The Influencers Formula®
The Five Tenets of Influence

Be Seen	Be Heard	Be Easy To Follow	Be The Solutuon	Be Paid
How do they find you?	How do they get to know you?	How do they say 'yes' to you?	How do you become the answer they're searching for?	How do you turn influence into income?

1

WHY THIS BOOK
AND WHO IT'S FOR

Donna Kunde

*There are people searching for you right now, for what you have to
offer. And if you are able to have those conversations with them —
which you will be able to when you follow our system — they will
tell you exactly what they are looking for, exactly what they need,
and exactly what they will pay.*

In the bustling world of podcasting, where millions of voices
compete for attention, many creators find themselves caught
in what we call the download trap. They wait for the numbers to grow before trusting their voice. They wait for external
validation before believing their work matters. They wait to feel
ready before allowing themselves to lead.

If you have ever found yourself refreshing analytics, wondering whether your show is "working," you are not alone. And I
want to tell you something important right from the start, your
podcast is already working, just not in the way you have been
taught to measure it.

The industry has convinced creators that success is about:

- Downloads
- Visibility
- Popularity
- Sponsorships
- Constant promotion

But those numbers rarely reflect the true value of your work or the real lives it touches. And the truth is, focusing on them can actually take you further away from the impact you could be making and the people you're here to serve.

You do not need permission to use your voice.
You do not need a certain number of listeners to matter.
You do not have to prove your worth to be heard.
Your voice is here for a reason. Someone is already searching for the perspective you carry.

Here is the shift that changes everything. Once you see it, the old model stops making sense.

THE PODCAST PROFIT SHIFT

What if your podcast is not the business, but the doorway into your business? Because when you stop trying to get paid by the industry and start getting paid by the people you are here to help, everything changes.

You stop broadcasting and start connecting. You stop chasing listeners and start serving clients. You stop performing and start leading.

This book is your roadmap for making that shift. It is built from real conversations with real podcasters across the world, from Lebanon to Singapore, Bangladesh to Vietnam, the United States to Australia, creators working in different industries, cultures, and economies, but all asking the same question: How do I turn my message into something that matters and something that lasts?

Not by becoming an influencer. Not by entertaining the masses. Not by running harder on the content treadmill. But by building a clear, human pathway for listeners to take the next step with you.

THE EFFICIENCY OF CONVERSION OVER AUDIENCE SIZE

We are not replacing one belief with another. We are choosing a more efficient business model.

A traditional sponsor-based podcast requires thousands of listeners to earn a small amount of revenue. For example, a typical ad rate pays between **$15 to $25 per 1,000 downloads**. To earn $1,000 from sponsorship alone, most podcasters would need:

40,000 to 70,000 downloads in one month.

Most independent podcasters never reach that level. And even those who do must repeat that work every month to maintain revenue.

The download model rewards constant content production and endless audience growth. It is built on volume, not depth.

By contrast, two clients at **$500** each generate the same $1,000. Those clients come through relationship, clarity, value, and invitation, not scale. Your podcast is not measured by reach. It is measured by connection.

This is why the Five Tenets and the 13-week System exist. They make connection reliable. They turn listeners into participants. They turn participants into clients. They allow you to grow through alignment instead of exhaustion.

You do not need a bigger audience.

You need a clearer pathway.

WHAT YOU WILL LEARN IN THESE PAGES

This is not a book about how to start a podcast. It is a book about how to:

- Be Seen as the trusted authority you already are
- Be Heard with clarity and confidence
- Be Easy to Follow so listeners know how to take the next step
- Be the Solution your audience is actively searching for
- Be Paid in alignment with your expertise and values

You need a system that allows your podcast to do what it does best: start the right conversations with the right people and lead them forward.

Your podcast is not just content; your podcast is a pathway. Your message is not something extra you add to your work; your message *is* the work. It is the heart of your business. Your message is the business.

This is where it begins.

2

WHERE TO START

Donna Kunde

Every book offers a promise. This one offers a process.

Your *Message Is the Business* is not meant to be read once and set aside. It is designed to be used, revisited, and applied as you grow. The ideas inside are part of a larger system—one that helps you turn your podcast and message into a sustainable business built on real influence.

The best way to begin is simple: start where you are.

You don't need to have everything figured out. You don't need a large audience or a detailed plan. You only need the willingness to look at your message in a new way and take one clear step forward.

As you move through these chapters, you'll see how each one builds upon the next. Some will inspire you to think differently. Others will give you practical tools to act immediately. Together, they will help you connect what you already have—your voice, your story, and your experience—to the business you're building.

Here's how to make the most of your time with this book:

1. **Pause often.** Take a moment after each chapter to reflect before moving on.
2. **Take notes.** Capture your ideas, examples, and next steps as they come.
3. **Apply what fits.** Every idea won't apply to everyone. Choose what serves your current stage and goals.
4. **Return as you grow.** This book will meet you differently each time you revisit it.

By the end, you'll understand not only how to turn your message into a business but also how to create lasting influence with purpose and clarity.

So, take a deep breath and begin. The first step is simply to keep reading.

3

THE FIVE TENETS OF INFLUENCE

Building Profitable Purpose Through Strategic Connection
Donna Kunde and James Bryant

Influence isn't built in a moment. It's built by showing up,
speaking clearly, leading simply, serving generously, and owning
your value, one tenet at a time.

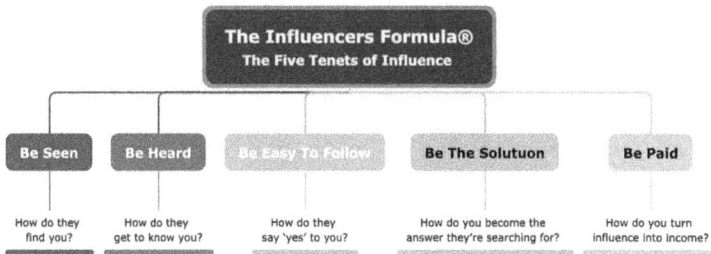

T he ideas in this chapter are drawn from the internationally best-selling book *The Influencers Formula*®, a foundational guide for coaches, consultants, and creators ready to build platforms rooted in clarity, connection, and purpose. These ideas were built in real time with real people asking real questions.

They still guide the work of influence-driven creators around the world. This is a framework that helps thought leaders step into profitable visibility without compromising their message.

Influence at its best isn't about persuasion or performance.

It is about serving the right people with clarity and value, in a way that feels aligned for everyone involved, and being compensated as a natural reflection of the transformation you provide.

Sarah stared at her laptop screen, scrolling through months of content she had created—blog posts, social media updates, podcast episodes, and email newsletters. An impressive body of work by any measure. Yet her bank account told a different story. Despite showing up consistently and putting out what she believed was meaningful work week after week, the momentum just wasn't there.

Does that sound familiar?

THE MOMENTUM PARADOX

This scenario plays out countless times across the entrepreneurial landscape. Passionate experts, talented creators, and dedicated professionals find themselves caught in what we call the momentum paradox: doing all the right things yet feeling perpetually stuck. They are visible and consistent, but the bridge between their expertise and sustainable income remains frustratingly elusive.

The problem is not effort. The problem is effectiveness. More specifically, it is the difference between chaotic presence and strategic presence. Anyone can hit publish. Anyone can show up. But transforming visibility into credibility, and structuring that credibility so it converts into measurable revenue, requires something intentional.

It requires a systematic framework designed to build profitable purpose through genuine human connection.

This is where the Five Tenets of Influence come into play. They are not a marketing checklist. They are a synchronized rhythm that moves people naturally from stranger to committed client.

Understanding the difference between linear tactics and rhythmic systems marks a fundamental shift in how we build influence in the modern marketplace.

Understanding Rhythmic Influence

Traditional marketing often presents influence-building as a linear progression: create content, build an audience, make offers, generate sales. Logical, but incomplete. Real influence does not develop in a straight line.

Influence functions more like an electrical circuit. Each component must work in harmony with the others. If any part of the circuit breaks, the current stops flowing. This is why you might generate traffic but struggle with conversions, or have a strong offer that no one discovers.

The Five Tenets of Influence — Be Seen, Be Heard, Be Easy to Follow, Be the Solution, and Be Paid with Purpose — operate as interconnected elements within this circuit of connection. They work in a continuous, synchronized rhythm. When applied with intention, this rhythm transforms exhausting hustle into a steady, predictable structure for sustainable growth.

Think of this framework as the foundation for building a profitable, purpose-driven business. Each tenet plays a precise role in moving someone from first discovering you to becoming an aligned, committed client.

Five Tenets of Influence as Building Blocks of Connection

Tenet One: Be Seen

This is the discovery mechanism. It is how your ideal clients first become aware of you. Be Seen is not passive. It is about placing yourself intentionally in the spaces where your ideal clients are already searching for solutions.

TENET TWO: BE HEARD

This is the connection mechanism. It is how people begin to feel understood by you. Be Heard requires language that reflects your audience's internal thoughts and lived experiences. When people hear their own challenges reflected back to them, trust begins.

TENET THREE: BE EASY TO FOLLOW

This governs the response mechanism. It is how someone takes the first small step toward working with you. Be Easy to Follow removes confusion, complexity, and decision fatigue. When the next step is simple and clear, more of the right people move forward.

TENET FOUR: BE THE SOLUTION

This is the trust mechanism. It aligns what you promise, how you deliver results, and the values that guide your work. When your promise, process, and purpose match, trust becomes a natural outcome.

TENET FIVE: BE PAID WITH PURPOSE

This is the relationship renewal mechanism. It ensures the way clients invest feels aligned with both your values and theirs. Being paid becomes a continuation of trust, not a disruption of it.

The effectiveness of this framework does not come from any one tenet alone. The power is in their synchronized rhythm. When all five work together, visibility feels natural, credibility grows organically, and revenue becomes a predictable result.

HOW THE SYSTEM COMES TO LIFE

Inside the Podcast Profit System, these Tenets come to life in two environments. The Lab provides the strategic foundation where your message becomes clear and your framework takes shape. The

Mastermind offers the lived experience of applying those ideas inside a supportive community. Together, these environments create the rhythm that transforms clarity into consistency and consistency into influence.

WHERE STRATEGY MEETS ALIGNMENT

The real advantage of this framework is alignment. When your message, methods, offers, and values all point in the same direction, your efforts begin to compound. Influence stops feeling like something you must push and starts feeling like something that moves with you.

The right people find you. The right clients stay. Your work becomes meaningful and profitable.

Influence is not about persuading or convincing. It is about serving the right people with clarity and integrity. It is about making it easy for them to understand how you help and inviting them into a relationship that supports their goals as well as your own.

FROM SHIFT TO PRACTICE

You have made the shift. You can see your podcast not as the business, but as the doorway into your business. You have learned what matters most, how the Five Tenets work together, and why connection rather than volume moves people forward.

Now we move from understanding to practice.

Influence grows when you apply one idea at a time in the right order and at a steady pace. You do not need to do everything. You only need to do the next right thing.

Part 2 begins with the first real edge most creators feel when they decide to step forward: being seen. Visibility brings courage and vulnerability to the same moment. We will make space for both.

From there, you will watch how a steady presence becomes authority. Not by pushing harder, but by aligning what you say with how you show up so people feel safe trusting your voice.

You already have what you need to begin. In the next section, we will help you practice it with clarity and rhythm.

With this companion resource, you will be able to evaluate your visibility, message, and client pathway from all three worlds we've discussed. Refer to the Five Tenets of Influence Primer as you move through this chapter: PodcastProfitSystem. com/message-book-resources.

WHAT ARE YOU DISCOVERING SO FAR?

_____

_____

_____

_____

_____

_____

_____

_____

_____

_____

_____

_____

_____

_____

_____

_____

_____

_____

_____

_____

If something in these pages made you pause, write, or highlight a line to return to later, would you take a moment to leave an honest review? Reviews help this message reach more podcasters who are searching for their next step.

PART II

BUILDING INFLUENCE

If Part I helped you see your podcast as the doorway into your business, Part II helps you step through it. This section shows you how influence is built from the inside out by strengthening one Tenet at a time, making space for courage, clarity, and authority to grow in steady, human ways. You will learn to work with what you already have, make friends with fear, and shape the kind of presence people trust and follow.

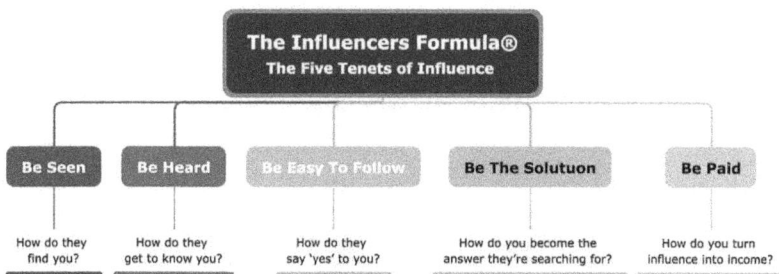

The Influencers Formula®
The Five Tenets of Influence

Be Seen	Be Heard	Be Easy To Follow	Be The Solutuon	Be Paid
How do they find you?	How do they get to know you?	How do they say 'yes' to you?	How do you become the answer they're searching for?	How do you turn influence into income?

4

HOW TO BEGIN WITHOUT STARTING OVER

Donna Kunde

Influence does not begin when everything is in place.
It begins when you decide to work with what you
already have.

The Five Tenets are not meant to be mastered all at once. Influence grows in layers, not leaps. The goal is not intensity. It is rhythm. You begin where you are, strengthen one area at a time, and the system becomes easier and more effective as you go.

STEP ONE — IDENTIFY YOUR STARTING TENET

Look at your current reality and choose one Tenet to focus on first.

If this is happening ...	Then focus on ...
You have lots of content but few people see it	*Be Seen*
People see you but do not engage	*Be Heard*

People engage but do not take the next step	*Be Easy to Follow*
People take steps but do not commit	*Be the Solution*
Interested prospects hesitate when it's time to invest	*Be Paid with Purpose*

This is not a test or a ranking. It is simply locating the leverage point—the place where one small improvement creates the greatest movement.

STEP TWO — REFLECT ON WHAT'S WORKING

Before fixing anything, notice what already works.
Where does your audience naturally respond?
Where do conversations flow easily?
Where do you feel most confident sharing your message?
These are signs that a Tenet is already strong. Your job isn't to rebuild everything from scratch—it's to steady what's already in motion.

STEP THREE — STRENGTHEN THE CONNECTION

Choose one small action that helps you express this Tenet more consistently. That might mean sharing your message more openly, clarifying an invitation, or simplifying the next step.
Consistency builds trust. Trust builds momentum. Every small improvement compounds over time.

STEP FOUR — REVISIT AS YOU GROW

Once you strengthen one Tenet, return to the list and choose another. Growth follows rhythm, not reinvention. The Five Tenets work together like a circuit of connection—each one amplifies the others. As you refine one, the rest begin to flow more easily.

Influence grows through consistency. Your message gathers strength through repetition. Clarity becomes easier. Trust becomes natural. Revenue becomes predictable. Purpose becomes lived, not stated.

You do not have to rush, force, or leap. You only need to continue the rhythm.

And as you step into that rhythm, something new begins to surface—the edge between visibility and vulnerability. The moment you start sharing your voice more boldly, fear often arises. Not as an enemy, but as a signal that you are entering new territory.

That is where we go next: learning to make friends with fear, so that being seen no longer feels like exposure but like alignment.

5

MAKING FRIENDS
WITH FEAR
(*BE SEEN*)

By Donna Kunde, Creator of the Podcast Profit System

The moment you decide to offer support instead of just giving it away is the moment you stop waiting to be ready and start walking in your purpose.

The vision board seemed innocent enough, just another creative exercise in a coaching course. But when Donna Kunde saw the line of microphones across the top of her carefully crafted collage, terror surfaced. Here was a woman who had lived most of her life as "the main character in a silent film," raised to be seen and not heard, shaped by environments where her voice simply did not matter. The microphones represented everything she feared most: being heard, taking up space, and trusting that she had something worth saying.

Yet something deeper stirred, a quiet recognition that the desire to speak was not random. At just over fifty years old, Donna faced a choice that would change not only her life but the lives of thousands of others to come. She could listen to the fear, or she could consider the possibility that the fear was simply an outdated signal, a warning designed for a world she no longer lived in.

A chance connection at a women's chamber event led to a friendship with a radio station general manager. When that station was sold in 2019, Donna and her colleague launched an internet radio station for business owners in January 2020, just months before the world shut down and people everywhere found themselves craving real human connection.

As colleagues and entrepreneurs suddenly lost work, Donna extended a simple invitation: "Would you like to have a radio show?" Forty-plus professionals from fourteen countries said yes. And almost immediately, the same questions echoed over and over, questions that would become the foundation of her signature teaching:

- What do I say?
- How do I structure this so it does not feel scattered?
- How do I talk about what I offer without feeling salesy?

In helping others answer those questions, Donna found her own voice. The system born from those first conversations, Business Podcasting Made Easy™, has now produced over 15,000 episodes and more than a million downloads. More importantly, it has given countless coaches, consultants, and entrepreneurs a way to speak naturally, clearly, and confidently about the work they feel called to do.

Her journey from silence to expression reflects a truth most of us have to learn. Fear is not the enemy. Fear is a protector that simply has not updated its instructions. *The same fear that once tried to keep you from being heard may now try to keep you from being paid. It is trying to protect you in a moment where you no longer need protection.*

THE RADICAL ACT OF MAKING FRIENDS WITH FEAR

Most personal development advice teaches that fear must be conquered, overridden, or pushed through. Donna offers a different perspective. What if fear is not the enemy at all, but a well-meaning protector that simply has not updated its job description?

"Fear is just trying to protect you," she explains, tracing the roots of internal resistance back to childhood. By the age of ten, most of us have heard "no" far more frequently than "yes." The parent who pulled us back from danger, the teacher who quieted our excitement, the relative who encouraged us to "tone it down," each moment formed neural pathways meant to keep us safe. But long after the original context has passed, those same pathways continue to fire.

The work is not to eliminate fear, but to speak to it. When the familiar stir of hesitation rises before hitting record, sharing a message publicly, or making an offer, Donna suggests asking yourself what the fear is trying to protect. Is the danger real? If you speak, if you share, if you show up, will you actually be unsafe? What is the true worst-case scenario, and could you handle it? This simple dialogue can turn fear from a barrier into information.

WHOSE VOICE ARE YOU REALLY HEARING?

One of the most meaningful shifts in Donna's approach comes from a simple question she asks her clients. Whose voice are you hearing?

When the familiar internal critic begins its litany of doubts:

- Who am I to charge for this?
- What if no one buys?
- What if they think I am only in it for the money?

We assume this voice is our own. But Donna challenges this.

More often than not, the voice of doubt did not originate with us. Babies are not born questioning their worth. Children speak, create, and offer naturally. Doubt is something we learn. It comes from the environments we were raised in, the adults who shaped us, the experiences that taught us to shrink or hold back. Someone, somewhere, handed us that voice. Which means it can be returned.

This realization is freeing. The hesitation to offer your work at a price is rarely about the work's value. It is a protective mechanism shaped long ago. Its purpose was to keep you safe. But safe is not the same as fulfilled.

Reclaiming your voice now includes reclaiming your right to earn from it.

And this is where expression begins to be something you allow yourself to be valued for.

THE THREE WAYS WE CREATE

Understanding how creation actually happens makes it easier to work through the moments when doubt, hesitation, or overwhelm show up. Donna describes the creative process as moving through three centers: the heart, the head, and the hands.

THE HEART HOLDS THE SPARK.

It is the feeling that you have something meaningful to say, the desire to help others, and the pull to express what you have lived and learned. This emotional current matters. Listeners can feel it even before they fully understand your message.

THE HEAD IS WHERE THE FRICTION APPEARS.

This is where the questions arise. Will this make sense? Is anyone listening? Am I doing this right? The head wants to protect you from mistakes and embarrassment, so it tries to take control.

This is also where the old voices of doubt and comparison tend to echo the loudest. The head is not the enemy, but it cannot lead.

THE HANDS ARE WHERE CREATION BECOMES REAL.

This is the moment you hit record, write the offer, schedule the social media posts, or publish the invitation. This is where ideas leave the mind and enter the world. Without this step, nothing changes.

When you begin offering support beyond free content, all three centers must come into alignment again. Not with force. With permission.

The heart says, "This matters."

The head responds, "Let's make it make sense."

The hands say, "Let's create it."

This alignment does not happen automatically. It requires attention, rhythm, and a structure that makes showing up feel natural rather than heavy. This is one of the reasons Business Podcasting Made Easy™ has been so effective. It provides the framework that keeps the heart inspired, the head organized, and the hands moving so your message does not stall before it is ever shared.

The Podcast Profit System™ continues this same approach by giving your message a path forward. It takes what you have already created and organizes it into a clear journey that leads somewhere meaningful, so your podcast becomes a system you can rely on rather than a task you must continually power yourself.

When all three work together, creating stops feeling like pushing uphill.

It starts feeling like expression—honest, grounded, and sustainable.

TAKING THE FIRST STEP

Once you recognize that fear is not a stop sign but a signal, something subtle shifts. You stop waiting to feel ready before making your offer. You offer because the support is ready. You offer because the listener is already searching.

Most people believe confidence comes first and action follows. But in practice, it happens the other way around. Confidence is built through use. A message deepens when it becomes a pathway. An offer becomes natural through repetition, not perfection.

You do not need to feel fearless to begin. You only need to feel willing.

Willing to let your work be received.

Willing to make space for someone to say yes.

Willing to trust that the same voice that guided your podcast can guide your offer, too.

You do not have to share everything all at once. You do not have to prove yourself. You only need to begin where you are—with one clear step, one honest invitation.

The first step is not about strategy. It is about permission.

Permission to be seen.

Permission to support.

Permission to receive.

Your offer is not an interruption.

It is part of the conversation you have already started.

It is where your listener moves from curiosity to commitment.

From content to change.

And if fear still lingers as you take that step, you are not doing it wrong.

You are doing it right.

This is what growth feels like.

Fear softens when you begin to move. What once felt like exposure begins to feel like expression. As you take the first steps to be seen, clarity starts to emerge—not all at once, but in moments. The more you show up, the more you see what truly resonates.

That's where we go next. You'll meet Mariette, a business owner who discovered that authority doesn't come from trying harder or being louder. It comes from alignment. Her journey shows what happens when fear gives way to rhythm—when your message becomes clear, your voice becomes steady, and your audience begins to trust you before you ever ask for a sale.

Because being seen isn't just about visibility. It's about allowing your message to stand where you once stood in fear.

6

BUILD YOUR AUTHORITY BLUEPRINT
(*BE THE SOLUTION*)

By Mariette Snyman, Host of Calm, Clear & Helpful Podcast

*Audiences today are smart, aren't they? They see through
the overly polished corporate veneer. They don't just connect
with credentials or job titles. They connect with people, with
vulnerability, with shared humanity.*

You are now beginning to build your presence as someone others look to for clarity and confidence. Not through force or performance, but through steadiness and alignment. The inner work you completed in Part I helped you see yourself differently, and the Alignment Compass helped you begin living that truth in small daily ways. Now we turn to how that inner steadiness becomes influence. In this chapter, Mariette shows how a calm, clear presence becomes the foundation of trust, connection, and authority. This is where your voice begins to feel safe to others because it has become safe to you.

Authority is not built by producing more content. It is built through strategic positioning that moves you from being another

29

podcaster to becoming the trusted voice people turn to. This is where the Five Tenets of Influence begin to do their work.

Mariette Snyman's thirty-year journalism career offers a clear example of how credibility grows when authenticity is supported by structure. In the crowded wellness landscape, she faced a question familiar to many podcasters.

How do you establish genuine authority without slipping into self-promotion?

The answer was not louder marketing or a more polished delivery. It came from something quieter and more disciplined. Her work was shaped by journalistic ethics, emotional intelligence, and a steady practice of telling true stories with clarity and care.

This chapter shows how one journalist built a platform that professionals trust. More importantly, it shows how you can apply the same principles to develop respected authority in your own field.

BUILDING THE FOUNDATION WITH CURIOSITY AND TRUST

At the center of this authority-building system is Mariette Snyman, a journalist with a thirty-year career grounded in understanding the human experience. Her work does not come from marketing theory or business frameworks. It comes from genuine curiosity about how people make meaning in their lives.

This curiosity is both personal and professional. Mariette's interviewing style has been shaped by lived experience. Childhood joy. Parenting. Career success accompanied by loss. Divorce followed by rediscovery. Grief alongside growth. This depth of self-awareness is not a side note - it is the source of her credibility. It allows her to ask questions that invite guests to share not only what they know, but who they are.

The evidence of this trust is visible. More than 160 health and wellness professionals from all over the world have chosen to collaborate with her platform and contribute meaningful educational content through articles or her weekly podcast, *Calm,*

Clear and Helpful. That number is more than a metric. It signals endorsement from a community that is cautious about media partnerships.

When professionals repeatedly choose to work with a journalist, it means something. They trust the editorial standards, the process, and the platform's intention. They know their expertise will be presented with care and reach the right audience in the right way.

WHERE MONEY ALIGNS WITH INTEGRITY

The platform operates on a sponsored content model, which naturally raises an important question: How do you maintain journalistic integrity when payment is involved? This tension sits at the center of modern media, and how the platform addresses it is part of what makes the system work.

The safeguard is what we call the journalistic integrity filter.

Only content that genuinely serves the audience and aligns with the platform's mission is accepted. This is not a slogan. It is an active editorial standard that protects the credibility of every feature, podcast episode, and written piece.

In practice, this means that if someone approaches with content that is primarily promotional, it does not move forward in its original form. The conversation shifts to what knowledge, insight, or lived experience will genuinely support the listener.

Editorial control remains with the journalist, not the advertiser.

This changes the nature of the exchange. The expert is not purchasing airtime. They are investing in the time, skill, and professional discernment required to present their work with clarity and integrity.

The mission statement reinforces the boundary. The content is educational and supportive, and it never replaces professional evaluation or clinical care. In the wellness field, where misinformation can cause real harm, this commitment is essential.

That responsibility extends beyond language. The platform includes contact information for national mental health support organizations such as the South African Depression and Anxiety Group and Akeso Helplines. This communicates something foundational:

They are not only discussing wellness.

They are participating in the ecosystem of care.

It is authority built through responsibility rather than performance.

DESIGNING AUTHORITY THROUGH AUDIO AND WRITING

What makes this authority model effective is its blend of audio and written content. Each format serves a distinct purpose, and together, they create a level of trust and credibility that neither could achieve alone.

The podcast is where trust begins.

When listeners hear an expert speak in a calm and thoughtful conversation, they do more than learn what the expert knows. They get a sense of who the expert is. Tone, presence, pacing, and personality come through in a way text alone cannot. This is especially important in wellness work, where trust is personal and relational.

The weekly podcast is available on major platforms, including Apple Podcasts, Spotify, Pocket Casts, Player FM, and Iono.fm. By meeting listeners where they already spend time, the platform creates easy, ongoing access to the expert's voice.

The written articles serve a different purpose.

They provide depth, structure, and the ability to return to ideas again and again. They allow readers to reflect, make notes, and share the expert's work with others. These articles are not transcripts. They are crafted features that highlight the expert's knowledge while also honoring the human story behind the work.

The real strength comes from how the two formats connect.

Podcast episode pages include links to related articles.

Articles link back to recorded conversations featuring the expert.

These formats complement each other.

Someone who discovers an article through search can listen to the expert's voice, if they have recorded an episode. Someone who begins with the podcast can move into related written material to explore ideas more deeply.

This creates multiple entry points for learning and connection, increasing engagement.

It is authority building that is natural, repeatable, and sustainable.

FINDING YOUR OWN WAY INTO AUTHORITY

Not every expert begins from the same place. Some are just starting to share their voice publicly. Others are growing into thought leadership. And some are ready to articulate a signature message with greater clarity and conviction. The authority-building system reflects this through three feature packages, offering different entry points depending on where someone is in their journey.

PATHWAY ONE

Focuses on personal connection. This approach emphasizes being known, not simply being correct. Experts have the opportunity to pair a podcast episode or topical article with a personal feature that introduces them as a whole human being. This builds trust quickly and allows people to understand the experiences, values, and lived perspectives that shape the expert's work.

PATHWAY TWO

Supports the development of thought leadership. This is for those ready to express their ideas more fully and more publicly. It combines an expertise-driven podcast episode with an inspirational written feature that explores the story behind the work, with add-on opportunities for expanded visibility. The emphasis is on the "why" that informs the "what," helping the audience connect to both the knowledge and its origins.

Pathway Three

Designed for moments when a message needs a specific frame or is intended for a specific platform. This pathway offers customized storytelling to align the message with the timing, audience, and impact the expert hopes to create.

Together, these pathways allow experts to enter the system at a point that matches their readiness, while also giving them room to grow into the next level of visibility and influence at a natural pace.

The Human Connection Formula

This approach to building authority rests on something simple and deeply human. People do not form trust based on credentials alone. They are looking for the person behind the expertise. They are looking for stories, lived experiences, honesty, and shared meaning.

This is why the platform uses two types of written features. The first is topical or evergreen content. These articles focus on practical, structured knowledge. They show the reader that the expert has mastery in their field. They answer real questions on topics like ADHD, functional medicine approaches, or techniques such as Brain Gym. These pieces quietly establish the expert as someone who knows what they are talking about.

The second type of article serves a different purpose. These are inspirational narratives that make the expert relatable. Instead of leading with credentials, they lead with humanity by offering a peek at the person behind the professional.

For example, one personal article, coupled with a podcast episode, shared the story of Dr. Arien. Her expertise was real, but her authority came alive when she spoke about finding ways to cope with depression and stroke. The power was not in a medical explanation. It was in the honesty of sharing her health challenges and how they transformed the way she serves others.

This is the heart of the Human Connection Formula. Expertise earns attention. Humanity earns trust. When both are present at the same time, authority becomes natural instead of manufactured.

THE PRODUCTION PROCESS

One of the strengths of this system is how it removes the pressure that often prevents experts from sharing what they know, especially when it comes to podcast guesting. The process is collaborative, steady, and guided. Instead of asking the expert to perform, it creates the conditions for real clarity and confidence.

The preparation begins with selecting topics that already matter to the audience. The journalist examines the questions people are asking and the challenges they face, then works with the expert to shape the conversation's angle. This ensures that the content is both relevant and grounded in the expert's true area of strength.

The question framework is what changes everything. The questions are crafted by a human interviewer who has conducted countless magazine and more than 300 podcast interviews. They are thoughtful, precise, and designed to reveal substance. Experts receive the questions in advance so they can reflect and prepare. This removes anxiety and allows them to bring their strongest stories, examples, and insights forward.

The recording happens either online or in person, always in a calm environment that encourages openness. There is no rush. Some conversations run 25 minutes. Some run for an hour. The pace is determined by the depth of the topic, not a script or time constraint.

Once the recording is complete, the expert's work is done. The platform handles the editing, mixing, and final production. This keeps the process clean and efficient for professionals who do not have time to learn audio engineering or manage distribution.

The result is content that feels natural and grounded. The expert sounds like themselves. And the audience can feel that.

THE TRANSFORMATION FROM RAW EXPERTISE TO POLISHED AUTHORITY

Concerning interviews for articles, the real shift happens when the initial conversation is crafted into a written piece that carries authority, clarity, and emotional resonance.

A raw transcript reflects how people speak. It includes incomplete thoughts, tangents, filler language, and small detours. The journalist studies this raw material to find the central ideas and the most meaningful moments. Then they arrange those ideas in a clear, logical sequence that guides the reader.

This is not simply correcting grammar or tightening sentences. It is translation. The goal is to preserve the expert's voice while shaping the message into a form that is strong, clear, and compelling page presence. The warmth and authenticity of spoken language become structured insight in written form.

The work is done by a human. It relies on judgment, empathy, and a deep understanding of how stories connect with readers. The choices of tone, pacing, and emphasis reflect professional experience, not algorithmic patterning. That distinction matters. It builds trust.

For inspirational feature articles, the process goes even deeper. The journalist begins by identifying the theme of the expert's journey. It could be resilience, transformation, identity, recovery, or renewal. The interview is then shaped to draw out the moments that illustrate that theme. The final piece offers encouragement through shared humanity. It shows not only what the expert knows, but who they are and what their experience means.

The result is not just an article. It is a piece of work that carries weight. It reflects the expert's character, conveys their credibility, and invites the audience to see themselves in the story.

THE CREDIBILITY COMPOUND EFFECT

One of the most powerful elements of this system is how authority continues to grow long after the initial podcast episode or article has been completed. This is more than exposure. It is an ongoing presence that builds trust over time.

The first stage provides the foundation: a professionally recorded podcast episode, a thoughtfully written feature article, a polished professional bio, and visible promotion through the platform's newsletter and social channels. These pieces establish credibility quickly.

The deeper value comes from what remains in place. Every time an expert is featured in an episode or article, the website page includes their photograph, bio, contact information, links to their work, and accompanying audio or written features. This page becomes a searchable home base that works quietly in the background for years. It is a reference point that clients, partners, and future media outlets can easily verify.

Podcast guests also receive an audio player they can embed on their own site. This brings a layer of third-party validation. It shows that someone outside their business has recognized and documented their expertise. This subtle endorsement carries weight.

The credibility continues to grow through ongoing promotion. The platform re-shares content and highlights new milestones such as book launches or awards. This steady visibility keeps the expert's work active in the public sphere without requiring them to constantly self-promote.

The result is authority that compounds. What begins as a single podcast episode or article becomes a permanent asset that attracts new opportunities over time. Instead of burning energy trying to stay visible, the expert's presence becomes continual, steady, and trusted.

THE LONG-TERM STRATEGY

Building authority is not a single moment. It grows when your voice is consistently present in the places where your audience learns, reflects, and makes decisions. In a world where content moves quickly and is just as quickly forgotten, one of the most valuable lessons from Mariette's approach is the emphasis on keeping meaningful work visible over time. A single interview or article can make an impression. But authority forms when that wisdom is encountered again and again.

This is why her system includes ongoing visibility. Previously published conversations are resurfaced and referenced. Stories are highlighted again when they become relevant to what is happening in the world. New achievements and milestones are added to existing pages to keep the expert's presence current.

This allows experts to remain visible even as they focus on the work itself. They do not need to create endless new content to maintain relevance. Their best work continues to speak for them.

The principle for podcasters is simple. Authority is sustained through continuity. Not volume. Not constant production. Steady, thoughtful presence.

When your voice remains in motion, your message continues to reach the people who need it.

THE BLUEPRINT REVEALED

What we have explored in this chapter is more than a model. It is a way of building authority rooted in trust, humanity, and consistency. These lessons apply whether you adopt a platform like Mariette's or shape your own approach. Authentic authority grows where expertise and lived experience meet. People connect not only to what you know, but to who you are and how you show up.

Using both audio and written formats strengthens that connection. Your voice builds familiarity. Your written content deepens understanding. Together, they help your message stay with people over time.

External validation also plays a role. When someone with credibility helps shape and share your message, it expands your authority. This is not about performing expertise. It is about being witnessed and reflected by someone who understands how to present your story with clarity and integrity.

Sustained visibility is what allows authority to grow. A single interview or article is a beginning, not the end. When your work continues to circulate, your leadership strengthens naturally without constant self-promotion.

At the center of all of this is authenticity. Authority that is forced or exaggerated will not hold. Authority that grows from lived experience, aligned values, and real work with real people becomes durable.

Now we shift toward application. You have begun shaping your Authority Blueprint. You have articulated who you are, what you stand for, and the transformation your work supports. The next step is to bring that clarity into the conversations you are already having. Authority develops in relationship. It takes shape in dialogue, through real human connection.

As you move into the next chapter, you will begin listening for the language your audience already uses. You will identify who is ready for the transformation you offer and align your work with the people who need it most. This is where your message becomes a pathway. When you know who you serve, the invitation becomes natural. When you speak directly to their needs, your podcast becomes a bridge. When you lead with clarity, engagement and revenue follow.

You are not trying to help everyone. You are choosing to help the right people in the right way. That is what authority looks like in practice.

You now have the beginnings of your Authority Blueprint. Authority does not live on the page. It becomes real when it reaches the people you are here to serve.

INTEGRATING WHAT YOU'VE BUILT

You've done the inner work. You've made friends with fear, clarified your message, and started building the authority that allows people to trust your voice. The systems you're creating now don't replace your humanity—they amplify it.

Like Mariette, you've seen how authority is less about performance and more about presence. It grows when you stay consistent, when your words match your values, and when your audience feels safe in your clarity.

Authority begins as belief. It becomes real through rhythm.

This completes the second part of your journey—**Building Influence**. You now have the foundation to move your message with confidence. The next step is learning how that message flows between worlds: your audience's world, your business's world, and the world where your future clients are already listening.

In the next section, we'll explore how your influence travels across these three spaces and how to strengthen the connections between them. You'll begin to see not just what you say or how you show up, but how your presence creates movement, trust, and transformation.

Because influence isn't built in isolation. It moves through conversations, relationships, and systems that carry your message farther than you could on your own.

This is where influence becomes action.

PART III

INFLUENCE IN ACTION

This is where your message begins to take shape in the real world. You start turning clarity into structure, intention into rhythm, and influence into simple pathways that help people move closer to the transformation they are seeking. It is the moment your podcast stops inspiring from a distance and starts guiding people forward in practical, grounded ways.

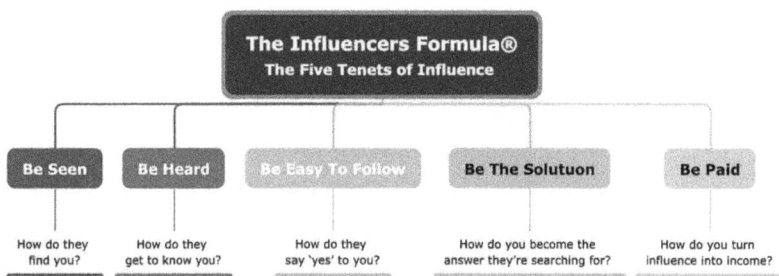

The Influencers Formula®
The Five Tenets of Influence

Be Seen	Be Heard	Be Easy To Follow	Be The Solutuon	Be Paid
How do they find you?	How do they get to know you?	How do they say 'yes' to you?	How do you become the answer they're searching for?	How do you turn influence into income?

Section A – Understanding Influence

This is where you begin to see your business the way your future clients see it. These chapters help you understand how your message moves through three different worlds: the moment someone discovers you, the moment they begin to trust you, and the moment they decide to take the next step. Once you see this flow clearly, every episode, offer, and system starts to feel like it belongs in the larger story you are building.

7

THE THREE WORLDS
OF INFLUENCE

Where Your Message Becomes a Business
Donna Kunde

*Influence expands when your message moves through
three worlds: how your audience experiences you, how you
show up consistently, and how your future clients step
forward with trust.*

I nfluence doesn't happen in one place. It grows as your message moves through three connected worlds—the listener's, your own, and your future client's. Together, they form the path from visibility to revenue. When you understand how these worlds work, you'll see where to focus your time and energy as your podcast becomes part of a real business.

The Three Worlds of Influence™ form your strategic framework. They help you see where influence begins, how it grows, and what connects each part of your message to the next. This is where you learn to think like a strategist, not just a content creator. Later, in Chapter 15, you'll explore the Podcast Profit

System™, which turns this strategy into practical, repeatable steps for building and monetizing your podcast business.

Most podcasters spend their days recording, publishing, and promoting without stopping to notice what's actually working. The three worlds bring clarity to that process. Each one shows you what to pay attention to and what to improve so your podcast does more than share your message. It starts to earn.

THE LISTENER'S WORLD — INFLUENCE ASSESSMENT

This is where it all begins. The listener's world is the space your audience already lives in their habits, searches, routines, and questions. Here, you're not creating. You're paying attention.

You listen for patterns in what people say, what they click on, and what keeps them coming back. You're learning how they hear you and what they believe you stand for. The goal isn't to talk more. It's to understand more deeply.

This part of the system is about **diagnosing influence**. You use the Five Dimensions of Influence™ to see how your audience experiences each of the Five Tenets: Be Seen, Be Heard, Be Easy to Follow, Be the Solution, and Be Paid with Purpose.

The insight you gather here is what shapes everything that follows. You'll start to see where trust already exists and where it quietly fades. That awareness helps you strengthen your message from the inside out.

YOUR WORLD — OFFER AND MESSAGE DEVELOPMENT

This is the space behind the microphone where clarity becomes opportunity. What you learn from your audience now helps you shape your offers and your message so they align with what people truly want and need.

In Your World, you use the Five Activators of Influence™ to turn what you already know into programs, products, and pathways your audience can follow. Each Activator ties back to one of the Tenets. Be Seen becomes strategic visibility. Be Heard becomes message clarity. Be Easy to Follow becomes a visible pathway. Be the Solution becomes your signature method. Be Paid with Purpose becomes a clear, values-based offer.

When you build your message this way, your podcast stops being just content. It becomes a bridge between what you teach and how people can work with you. That's when your message starts to generate real income and impact.

THE FUTURE CLIENT'S WORLD — SALES FUNNEL AND FLOW

This world is where connection becomes commitment. It's where your influence turns into income through systems that are simple, ethical, and aligned with the people you serve.

Here, you apply the Five Conversion Catalysts™ to design a smooth experience that guides listeners toward the right next step. You're not pushing for sales. You're creating confidence.

When your audience understands your process and feels safe in their decision, they move forward naturally. That's what a true funnel does. It makes it easy for someone who's already interested to take action without pressure.

Over time, this world starts working for you. Your systems nurture relationships, your message keeps moving, and your business keeps earning even when you're not behind the mic.

HOW THE WORLDS WORK TOGETHER

The three worlds move in a natural rhythm.

You listen and diagnose in the Listener's World.

You develop offers and structure in Your World.

You deliver results and create revenue in the Future Client's World.

Each one builds on the others. When you listen well, your offers improve. When your offers are clear, your funnel flows.

When your funnel works, you receive more feedback to refine what's next.

That rhythm keeps your message alive. It keeps you grounded, growing, and aligned with the people you serve.

PUTTING IT INTO PRACTICE

Take a few minutes to map your three worlds.

1. In the **Listener's World**, write one insight you've gained from your audience recently.
2. In **Your World**, note one offer or idea that grew from that insight.
3. In the **Future Client's World**, identify one next step you could make easier for your listeners today.

You don't have to fix everything or build a full system overnight. You only need to see where you are right now. Every layer of influence begins with awareness, alignment, and one small, deliberate step forward.

8

HOW YOUR AUDIENCE REALLY SEES YOU

The Listener's World of Influence
Donna Kunde

You cannot strengthen what you have not yet seen clearly.
Real influence begins with perspective.

Real influence starts with understanding. Before you try to grow your audience or improve your offers, you need to know how your message is being received.

The Listener's World is the first stage of your monetization system. It's where you stop guessing about what your audience wants and start listening for what they actually need. This stage helps you see which of the Five Tenets (Be Seen, Be Heard, Be Easy to Follow, Be the Solution, and Be Paid with Purpose) are strong and which need attention. The goal isn't to fix everything at once, but to understand how people experience you and your message.

SEEING THROUGH THEIR EYES

Every listener brings their own world into the conversation: what they're searching for, what they believe, and what they've already tried. You can't control that, but you can learn from it.

Ask yourself:

- What do they believe I can help them with?
- What problem do they think I solve?
- What are they still unsure about?

These questions reveal how clearly your message connects. When you understand what your audience already believes, you can meet them where they are and guide them toward what comes next.

THE FIVE DIMENSIONS OF INFLUENCE

The Five Dimensions of Influence help you see your message the way your audience experiences it. Think of them as five lenses that bring clarity to how your Tenets show up in real life.

VISIBILITY

Can the right people find you easily?
Visibility isn't about being everywhere. It's about showing up where your people are already looking for help. Think of it as being discoverable in the right places, the spots where your message naturally meets their needs.

RESONANCE

Do your words sound like their words?
Resonance happens when your message sounds like home to the person hearing it. When they recognize themselves in your stories or examples, they trust you.

CLARITY

Can they explain what you do in one sentence?

Clarity creates calm. When someone understands what you offer without having to work hard to figure it out, they feel relief. That's what makes them want to keep listening or take the next step with you.

AUTHENTICITY

Does your presence match your promise?

Authenticity is when what people hear from you feels true. It's not something you have to perform. It shows up naturally when your words, tone, and actions line up with what you believe and how you serve.

CONVERSION READINESS

Do they know what happens next?

This is where clarity meets invitation. When your audience knows what to do after listening, reading, or watching, they feel confident. Your next step doesn't have to be big; it just has to be clear and kind.

LISTENING FOR INSIGHT

You learn the most when you listen closely. Every comment, question, and silence carries information. Notice which topics spark energy, which stories people repeat, and which ones drift by unnoticed. That's your feedback loop.

You don't need complex analytics. Just listen for patterns. The more you understand what your audience values, the easier it becomes to align your content, offers, and conversations with what they already care about.

Each of these five dimensions helps you see what's really happening between your message and your audience. When you listen through these lenses, you start noticing what's working and what's waiting to grow.

PUTTING IT INTO PRACTICE

Choose one recent episode, post, or email and look at it through the Five Dimensions of Influence.

Ask yourself:

- Could the right people easily find this?
- Does it sound like their language or mine?
- Would they understand what happens next?
- Does it feel true to who I am?
- Is there a clear next step?

Write down what you notice, but resist the urge to fix it all right now. Seeing clearly is the first step. Awareness always comes before change.

In the next chapter, you'll learn how to bring structure and rhythm to what you've discovered here. You'll explore the Activators of Influence™, the systems that help you stay visible, consistent, and confident as your message grows.

9

WHEN EVERY POST
HAS A PURPOSE

Your World of Influence
Donna Kunde

When your message supports your offer, every piece of content
moves your business forward.

The second stage of this system is Your World. This is where you begin creating again, but with a newfound clarity and intention. You've already spent time listening and learning what your audience sees, hears, and wants. Now, you take what you've discovered and turn it into something tangible: content and offers that connect naturally and work together.

This world is about rhythm and purpose. It's where ideas take shape and your message finds direction through podcast episodes, social media posts, blogs, and calls to action that all serve a shared goal.

The Five Activators of Influence™ help you bring that rhythm to life. They guide you through two essential processes: creating or refining your offers so they align with what your audience truly needs, and building a content strategy that supports those offers across every platform.

When you work this way, your message feels alive. It reaches the right people, at the right time, with the right invitation. Each piece of content fits into a bigger picture, one that builds connection, trust, and forward movement for your business.

CONTENT THAT CONNECTS AND CONVERTS

Your content should make it easy for people to take the next step. That begins with clarity.

When you understand what your audience wants and how your offer helps, your content becomes a bridge. Every story, insight, and post points back to what you can help them achieve.

Think of your content as a conversation that unfolds over time. Each episode, post, or email adds another piece to that relationship. When your message connects to your offer, your audience doesn't feel sold to. They feel understood.

This is how influence begins to create income. You're not chasing followers or fighting algorithms. You're creating meaningful content that leads somewhere real.

THE FIVE ACTIVATORS OF INFLUENCE

Think of the Five Activators of Influence™ as the way you bring your Tenets to life. They keep your message grounded, your rhythm steady, and your results aligned with your purpose.

VISIBILITY RHYTHM

(Supports Be Seen)
Visibility is about rhythm, not reach. When you show up consistently in the few places where your audience already spends time, people begin to look for you there. Predictability builds recognition, and recognition builds trust..

MESSAGE ARCHITECTURE

(Supports Be Heard)

A clear message feels like a through-line that runs through everything you share. When your promise and your main topics stay aligned, your audience starts to recognize your voice before they even see your name.

PATHWAYS AND INVITATIONS

(Supports Be Easy to Follow)

People want to take the next step with you, but they need to see where to go. Add gentle invitations that make the path simple and obvious. When the next step is easy, progress feels natural.

SIGNATURE FRAMEWORK

(Supports Be the Solution)

Your framework is how you make your process visible. Breaking your method into clear, teachable steps shows people what's possible and how you can help. It also gives you language to talk about your work with confidence.

OFFER READINESS CONTENT

(Supports Be Paid with Purpose)

Before someone says yes, they need time to believe the change you promise is real for them. Share stories, examples, and insights that build that belief. When they finally reach your offer, it feels like the natural next step.

These five Activators keep your content grounded in purpose. Each one aligns your message and offers so that every post, episode, or email moves your audience—and your business—forward.

Making It Work for You

The Activators give your content direction. Instead of wondering what to post next, ask yourself, "Which Activator am I supporting today?"

That question keeps your focus steady. It turns content creation into a strategy instead of a guessing game.

This world isn't about producing more. It's about creating with purpose. When your offers and your content work together, your audience moves forward naturally.

When your offers lead, your message becomes clear. When your message supports your offers, your audience stays connected. That's how influence turns into sustainable income.

Putting It into Practice

Look at one recent episode, blog, or post and ask yourself:

- Which offer does this support?
- Which Activator does it align with?
- What clear next step am I giving my audience?

If the answers aren't clear, adjust your content until they are.

Every time you publish, you're either building momentum or slowing it down.

In the next chapter, you'll enter the Future Client's World and learn how to turn connection into commitment through simple, ethical funnels that guide your listeners from awareness to action.

10

TURNING LISTENERS INTO CLIENTS

The Future Client's World
Donna Kunde

Selling is simply continuing the conversation with clarity,
trust, and purpose.

The Future Client's World is where everything you've built begins to work together. You've listened to your audience. You've created meaningful content and offers that meet their needs. Now it's time to guide them through a clear, confident path that helps them take the next step.

This world is not about pressure. It's about process. When your systems are steady, your message moves on its own. You stop repeating the same conversations and start nurturing real relationships that grow naturally over time.

The goal of this world is simple: to make the journey from listener to client seamless and respectful. When your offers and your automation are aligned, every part of your business supports connection, not confusion.

FROM INTEREST TO ACTION

When someone listens to your podcast or engages with your content, they're already saying, "I'm curious." Your job is to turn that curiosity into confidence.

A well-designed funnel doesn't rush that process. It creates small, meaningful steps that help people make informed decisions. A clear pathway feels safe, predictable, and aligned.

This is how your systems become an extension of your message. They reflect your values, your rhythm, and your commitment to serve.

You're not creating a machine that replaces you. You're building a structure that carries your message farther than you could alone.

THE FIVE CONVERSION CATALYSTS

Each Catalyst reflects a simple, natural step in how people move from awareness to commitment. Together, they create a rhythm of trust that leads to action at the right time.

ATTRACT

Attraction begins with clarity. Help your audience see themselves in your message by speaking directly to the problem you solve and the transformation you guide. People are drawn to relevance, not reach.

ENGAGE

Show up with genuine value. Offer insights that teach, encourage, or affirm what your audience already feels. Engagement isn't about volume. It's about creating moments of connection that build familiarity and trust.

LEAD

Invite one simple next step. It might be downloading a guide, joining your email list, or scheduling a short call. Then deliver a small, meaningful win that shows your process works.

NURTURE

Keep showing up with empathy and insight. Let your emails, podcast episodes, and posts sound like your real voice—calm, consistent, and caring. This is where belief grows. Your audience starts to trust that the change you talk about can be real for them.

CONVERT

When the moment feels right, extend the invitation. Make it easy to say yes with a clear process and a simple offer. Conversion done well feels like alignment, not persuasion.

Each Catalyst strengthens the one before it. Attraction sparks interest. Engagement deepens trust. Leadership creates movement. Nurture builds readiness. And conversion completes the story. When these pieces work together, selling no longer feels like pressure. It feels like a partnership.

BUILDING A FUNNEL THAT FEELS HUMAN

A good funnel doesn't manipulate people. It mentors them through a process of understanding.

It helps people make the best decision for themselves. Sometimes that decision isn't "yes" today.

Every message, page, and email plays a part in this ongoing conversation. Each touchpoint either deepens trust or distracts from it.

When designing your funnel, consider what your audience needs to know, feel, and believe at each step. Guide them gently from interest to understanding, and from understanding to action.

Your nurture sequence isn't about selling. It's about helping people feel ready and confident to take the next step when the time is right.

MAKING THE SYSTEM WORK FOR YOU

The Future Client's World brings structure that replaces strain. When your funnels and nurture sequences are in place, they keep your message moving while you focus on your best work.

That consistency gives you freedom. Your podcast episodes, your emails, and your content all start to work together as one.

When someone listens, they know what to do next. When they visit your site, they know where to go. When they read your emails, they feel guided, not pushed.

That's when your message begins to carry its own momentum.

This is how influence becomes income with integrity. Your systems amplify your service. Your message becomes measurable. Your results become repeatable.

PUTTING IT INTO PRACTICE

Look at one of your current offers and ask yourself:

- What is the first step someone takes after hearing about it?
- How am I guiding that step with clarity?
- What support or follow-up keeps the conversation alive?
- Where could my system be smoother or more personal?

Start by refining one piece of your funnel, such as a single email, landing page, or follow-up message.

The goal is not to build everything at once. It's to build something that feels natural and trustworthy from start to finish.

When your systems, offers, and message work in harmony, you stop chasing sales and start creating steady, reliable growth.

FROM INFLUENCE TO INCOME

You now understand how influence moves.

It begins in your listener's world, where clarity and empathy open the door.

It continues in your world, where systems and rhythm give your message consistency.

And it culminates in your future client's world, where trust becomes the foundation for action.

This is how authority grows quietly, steadily, and with integrity. You no longer need to chase attention or force momentum. Your message is already doing the work.

What comes next is the natural progression of that influence. In the next section, we'll explore how to turn these conversations into sustainable revenue through structures that honor your message and serve your audience.

You'll learn how to align your podcast, your offers, and your systems so that every piece of your work leads somewhere meaningful—for you and for the people you're here to help.

The shift ahead is simple but profound.

You're no longer building influence for its own sake.

You're building it for impact and for income that reflects your true value.

WHAT ARE YOU DISCOVERING SO FAR?

_____

_____

_____

_____

_____

_____

_____

_____

_____

_____

_____

_____

_____

_____

_____

_____

_____

_____

_____

If something in these pages made you pause, write, or highlight a line to return to later, would you take a moment to leave an honest review? Reviews help this message reach more podcasters who are searching for their next step.

GET THE TOOLS THAT BRING THIS BOOK TO LIFE

SCAN ME

SCAN TO ACCESS YOUR BOOK BONUSES AND START PUTTING THE PODCAST PROFIT SYSTEM INTO ACTION..

SECTION B – EXPRESSING INFLUENCE

This is the moment your influence takes shape in the real world. Your stories, your voice, and your beliefs about value begin to guide how people experience you and how they choose to grow with you. These chapters help you show up with clarity and heart so income becomes a reflection of the transformation you create.

11

CLARITY CREATES CONNECTION
(BE EASY TO FOLLOW)

*By Kevin L. Beers, Bertram G. Robinson Sr, and Michael A.
Grant Jr., Hosts of the Survival Mode Podcast*

*Your vision will tell you who you want to serve. Your research
and your due diligence will tell you who you will best serve.*

The phone call came on a Tuesday afternoon. Dwayne, a
frustrated Gen Z entrepreneur, had reached his breaking
point. Despite having a solid business idea and the drive
to succeed, he couldn't figure out who his customers were.

"I feel like I'm throwing darts in the dark," he confessed
during our conversation. "Everyone says I need to find my target
market, but how do I actually do that?"

Dwayne's frustration echoes the struggles of countless entrepreneurs who find themselves stuck in what we call *marketing
limbo*—that uncomfortable space between having a great idea and
actually connecting with the people who need what you're offering.

The truth is, marketing isn't just about creating flashy adver-
tisements or posting on social media. It's about understanding the
fundamental relationship between your vision, your capabilities,

and the real people who will benefit from your products or services.

In today's hyper-connected yet paradoxically fragmented marketplace, the challenge is reaching the *right* people with the *right* message at the *right* time.

This chapter will guide you through the essential process of transforming your business vision into a targeted marketing strategy that actually works.

UNDERSTANDING YOUR TARGET AUDIENCE

The foundation of effective marketing begins with a fundamental question that many entrepreneurs get wrong. *Who is my target audience?* Most business owners approach this question by creating fictional personas based on age, income, and geographic location. While demographics matter, they're only part of the equation.

The real question you need to ask is more nuanced. *Who can I best serve, and who do I actually have access to?* This dual consideration forms the cornerstone of practical target market identification.

Consider the financial services industry, where the ideal client might be someone with substantial wealth who needs guidance in managing their assets. Billionaires certainly fit this description; they have money and often hire professionals to help manage it. However, the critical question becomes: Do you actually have access to billionaires? For most entrepreneurs starting out, the answer is no.

This is where the intersection of aspiration and reality becomes crucial. You might dream of serving high-net-worth individuals, but if your actual network consists primarily of middle-class professionals, that's where you need to focus your initial efforts. This doesn't mean abandoning your bigger aspirations; it means building your business on a foundation of accessible, serviceable customers while positioning yourself for future growth.

The access principle applies across industries. If you're in a rural area planning to sell life insurance, your primary market might be farmers and remote workers who choose rural living. If you're in an urban environment, you'll have access to a different demographic entirely. The key is honestly assessing your current reach while building systems to strategically expand it.

Geographic location plays a significant role in this assessment. Your physical location, your network's geographic distribution, and your delivery capabilities all influence who you can realistically serve. A local bakery has different access patterns than an e-commerce business, and your marketing strategy must reflect these realities.

Industry-specific considerations also matter tremendously. A B2B software company serving enterprise clients needs different access strategies than a consumer goods company targeting individual buyers. The complexity of your sales cycle, your customers' decision-making process, and the relationship-building requirements all influence how you define and reach your target market.

ALIGNING VISION WITH MARKET REALITY

The most successful marketing strategies emerge from carefully aligning your business vision with market realities. Your vision tells you who you want to serve and why your business exists. Your research tells you who you can actually serve effectively, given your current resources and market position.

This alignment process requires honest self-assessment and strategic thinking. Your vision should guide your market selection, but it should not blind you to practical constraints or unexpected opportunities that might not perfectly match your original ideas.

Consider a web design company that could technically serve any business needing a website. However, by focusing specifically on churches, the company creates a unique value proposition. Churches have specific needs that general business websites do not address, such as event management, sermon archives, donation processing, community-building features, and organization of spiritual content.

By aligning their vision with this specific market segment, the web design company can develop specialized expertise, create targeted marketing messages, and build a reputation within a defined community. When a church asks what makes them different from other web designers, they can tell a specific story about how they understand church needs and solve church-specific problems.

This specialization strategy, often called niche marketing, allows businesses to become the preferred provider within a specific segment rather than competing as a generalist in a crowded marketplace. The key is choosing a niche that aligns with your vision while offering sufficient market size and growth potential.

Your vision also influences how you communicate with your target market. If your vision emphasizes quality and craftsmanship, your marketing messages should reflect those values and target customers who prioritize quality over price. If your vision focuses on accessibility and affordability, your targeting and messaging should align with those priorities.

The alignment process is not static; it evolves as your business grows and your understanding of the market deepens. Early in your business development, you might focus on a narrow niche to establish credibility and generate initial revenue. As you grow, you can expand into adjacent markets while maintaining the core vision that drives your business.

Setting Clear and Measurable Marketing Goals

Effective marketing requires clear objectives that guide your strategy and allow you to measure what is actually working. Without specific goals, marketing becomes an expensive guessing game. Your goals determine the strategies you use, the content you create, and the metrics that matter most for your business.

Think of marketing goals like target practice. You need to know what you are aiming at and whether you hit it. Different goals require different approaches, tools, and messages.

Most marketing goals fall into four categories:

BRAND AWARENESS

These campaigns aim to expand your visibility. They measure reach, impressions, brand recognition, and social engagement. The question they answer is: Are more of the right people seeing you?

LEAD GENERATION

These campaigns focus on attracting people who have the potential to become customers. They measure click-through rates, landing page conversions, cost per lead, and lead quality. The question they answer is: Are the right people entering your world?

SALES

These campaigns focus on direct revenue. They measure conversion rate, average order value, customer acquisition cost, and return on ad spend. The question they answer is: Are your efforts generating income?

CUSTOMER RETENTION

These campaigns focus on increasing lifetime value. They measure repeat purchase rate, retention percentages, customer satisfaction, and churn. The question they answer is: Are you keeping the customers you worked so hard to acquire?

Before you launch any campaign, establish a clear baseline. Know where you are beginning. As campaigns run, track your progress consistently. Monthly or quarterly reviews help you identify trends early and make adjustments before problems grow. Small refinements in audience targeting, messaging, or budget allocation often make the biggest difference over time.

It is important to remember that marketing results often lag behind marketing activity. Some outcomes take weeks or months to show up, especially if your business has a longer sales cycle. Patience and consistency matter more than chasing quick wins or constantly changing tactics.

The most successful entrepreneurs treat marketing as a continuous learning process. Clear goals, consistent measurement, and simple adjustments turn marketing into a reliable system instead of a guessing game. When your goals align with your vision and you communicate value clearly, marketing becomes a sustainable engine for growth.

CLARITY CREATES CONNECTION. CONNECTION CREATES CHOICE.

You now have one ideal client you can clearly name, one core problem they want solved now, one offer direction that feels aligned, and one metric that tells you whether your effort is working. This clarity is not the end of your strategy. It is the beginning of your business.

When you know who you serve and why your work matters, your podcast stops being just content. It becomes a pathway. It becomes a way for people to recognize themselves in your message and make grounded decisions about their next step with you.

Be Easy to Follow is about simplicity, not shortcuts. Clarity opens the path, but Be Heard brings it to life.

In the next chapter, you will see how your story turns clarity into connection. It transforms understanding into trust and trust into movement. When people feel seen in your story, they no longer need to be convinced. They choose to walk with you.

12

STORIES MATTER
(BE HEARD)

By Gayle Turner and Shelli Jost Brady, Co-Hosts of the Stories
Matter!: Helping Leaders Transform Lives Podcast

Our customer is the hero. Our products, our services are there
to help our customer be the hero in achieving their destiny,
their glory, their impossible dream.

I n a business culture obsessed with metrics and measurement, two seasoned professionals came together to explore what clarity alone cannot deliver: the emotional power of story. Stories are the lifeblood of every successful organization. Gayle Turner of The Storytellers Channel and Shelli Jost Brady of Alchemy Consulting have spent decades helping leaders, founders, and creators understand that narrative is not something you add to your work later; it is the heart of how your work connects. Stories shape how people trust you, how they decide whether you understand them, and whether they feel safe enough to take the next step with you.

Their conversation revealed a profound insight that challenges a lot of conventional business advice. While many entrepreneurs focus on describing their services, showcasing their expertise, or refining their offers, the businesses that truly resonate understand something deeper: they're not in the business of selling products or services; they're in the business of helping heroes move through their journeys.

Every client arrives in the middle of their own story, a story about where they are, where they want to go, and what stands in the way. Your role is not to be the hero of that story. Your role is to be the guide. The one who says, I see where you are. I know this terrain. Let's walk it together.

This is the heart of Stories Matter. It's not about performance. It's not about persuasion. It's not about trying to impress anyone. It's about honoring the path someone is already walking and helping them continue it with more clarity, courage, and dignity.

THE STORY BENEATH THE BUSINESS

Every business, whether a one-person consultancy or a 10,000-person organization, is built on a foundational story: who we are, why we exist, who we serve, and what we believe is possible. But here is where many small businesses get stuck. They try to explain what they do before they ever connect with the person they're speaking to.

People don't connect through logic first; they connect through meaning. A client needs to hear themselves in your words before they can trust your expertise. They need to feel understood before they can feel guided. Which means the first task is not clarity of offering, it is clarity of story.

THE INTEGRATION OF STORY ACROSS ALL BUSINESS FUNCTIONS

The most successful organizations don't treat storytelling as a marketing function or communication technique. They recognize it as the fundamental way humans make sense of their experiences and make decisions. This understanding transforms how they approach every aspect of their business, from strategic planning to daily operations.

When employees understand and believe in the stories their organization tells about its mission, values, and impact, they become authentic ambassadors for those narratives. When suppliers and partners share similar stories about quality, integrity, and mutual success, business relationships become more resilient and productive. When community members see the organization as a positive contributor to their shared story, they support one another during challenging times and celebrate successes.

The key is ensuring that all these stories are authentic and aligned. Customers quickly detect when there's a disconnect between the story an organization tells about itself and the reality they experience.

Employees become cynical when leadership espouses values that aren't reflected in actual policies and decisions. Partners lose trust when promises aren't kept and commitments aren't honored.

But when stories are authentic and consistent across all constituencies, something meaningful happens. The organization develops narrative coherence, a clear and believable story about who they are, what they do, and why it matters. This coherence becomes a competitive advantage because it enables faster decision-making, stronger relationships, and more effective communication at every level.

The businesses that master this approach don't just succeed financially. They create a lasting impact on everyone they touch. They become the kind of organizations where people want to work, where customers feel proud to be associated with the brand, where suppliers compete to earn partnership status, and where communities celebrate their presence and growth.

STORY SHAPES CULTURE AND CLIENT EXPERIENCE

The culture of your business, whether it is just you, or you and a small team, or a wider circle of collaborators, is built from the stories you tell about the work. Stories like:

- Why you show up the way you do
- What you believe is possible for the people you serve
- What you know from your own lived experiences
- What you've had to learn the hard way

These stories teach your clients how to be in relationship with you. When your story is grounded, authentic, and coherent, your business becomes easier to talk about, easier for people to trust, and easier for the right clients to choose, not because you have a perfect elevator pitch, but because your story feels true.

WHERE THIS MEETS PODCASTING

A podcast is not just a marketing channel. It is a storytelling space. Listeners don't press play because they are bored. They press play because they are searching:

- For direction
- For resonance
- For language for something they have felt but not yet named
- For someone who can walk with them

Your job as a host is not to prove expertise. It is to meet them in their story. A podcast becomes powerful, even profitable, not by reaching more people, but by reaching the right people more deeply. You are not gathering an audience. You are nurturing a relationship.

Your podcast is not the business. Your podcast is the doorway into your business. Your message, the story you are here to tell, that is the business.

THE PERSONAL LAYER THAT MAKES THIS HARD

Story is what allows your message to be heard, not just understood. When people can see their own hopes and struggles reflected in your words, they begin to trust you. That trust is the bridge between being heard and being chosen.

Be Heard helps you build connection. *Be Paid with Purpose* helps you honor that connection through fair and meaningful exchange. One allows your audience to feel seen. The other allows both of you to grow.

In the next chapter, you will explore how the stories you believe about money shape what you allow yourself to receive. It is not about learning to sell more. It is about learning to value what your work creates, and to let that value return to you.

13

REWRITE YOUR WEALTH STORY
(BE PAID WITH PURPOSE)

*By Raj Kapur, Founder of OptionsAhead.com and
Host of the Guidance to Wealth Podcast*

*Unless you believe you are worth more, you will generally get
in life what you think you are worth. And you know what, your
mindset determines that. Whether you are aware of it or not.*

O nce you have made space for your voice and learned to
move with fear rather than against it, another barrier
often arises. The barrier is not tied to speaking but to
receiving. You can share your message with confidence and even
make an invitation with clarity, yet something may still tighten
when it is time to be paid for your work.

This is where the conversation shifts from expression to worth.
You can master every podcasting and communication technique.
But if your relationship with money is tangled, monetization will
feel effortful, uncomfortable, or out of reach.

The statistics are sobering:

- The average coach earns only in the lower five-figure range

- Seasoned professionals with fifteen or more years of experience average around $120,000
- Most new coaches struggle to make ends meet
- All of this exists in an industry that has grown into a billion-dollar market

If the demand is there, and the industry is thriving, why are so many talented, certified coaches barely scraping by?

After interviewing hundreds of coaches and consultants across all experience levels, a clear pattern emerged. The difference between those earning five figures and those commanding six, seven, or even eight figures was not their education, certifications, or networking abilities. The fundamental distinction was something far more foundational: their wealth mindset.

This revelation challenges everything most coaches believe about building a successful practice. While many focus on learning new techniques, attracting more clients, or giving away free sessions to build their reputation, they are missing the critical foundation that determines whether any of these strategies will create lasting financial success.

UNDERSTANDING THE WEALTH MINDSET FOUNDATION

According to Raj, a wealth mindset includes the beliefs, habits, behaviors, and attitudes that separate those who build wealth from those who struggle with it. It is not about wishful thinking or vague positivity. It is about retraining how you see money, value, and your own worth in the marketplace.

Most coaches already possess a growth mindset. That is what drew them to personal development in the first place. But many are unaware that their subconscious beliefs about money are silently undermining their business. They keep showing up and keep giving value, but without understanding why it never fully adds up.

When successful people are asked what truly made the difference, the most consistent answer is mindset. Not strategy. Not credentials. Not luck. Mindset.

This truth applies not only to coaches, but to professionals in every field where financial growth and long-term sustainability matter.

A wealth mindset includes the ability to:

- Save money with intention
- Invest with discernment
- Improve your financial standing consistently
- Manage risk with perspective, not fear

The good news? This mindset can be developed. No matter your past income, upbringing, or financial literacy, these skills can be learned. **What matters most is the willingness to see differently and to begin.**

Recognizing the Poor Mindset Trap

The opposite of a wealthy mindset is what Raj calls a poor mindset. Most people who hold these beliefs have no idea they do.

This unconscious programming works like a financial thermostat. It automatically adjusts your income and opportunities to match your internal sense of worth, not your talent, your effort, or your potential.

Common poor mindset beliefs include:

- Thinking that making money is wrong or unethical
- Believing that earning income without physical labor means you do not deserve it
- Feeling convinced that you will never escape debt
- Assuming you lack the skills for financial success
- Remaining financially illiterate about cash flow, even as a business owner

These beliefs do not remain passive. They actively interfere with financial goals and push back on wealth-building opportunities. Like a computer program running quietly in the background, they sabotage your best efforts while your conscious mind stays busy with to-do lists and surface-level strategies.

Raj has seen this repeatedly. The coach who delivers powerful transformation but charges fees that barely cover expenses. The consultant who generates results but avoids fee discussions and gives away time in the name of "relationship building."

These patterns are not about pricing scripts. They come from deep internal wealth wounds. No marketing tactic can solve them until they are brought into awareness.

A Personal Journey from Limitation to Abundance

For many years, Raj believed the only way to increase income was to work harder. The idea of earning six figures felt out of reach. Growing up, he had never seen examples of wealth that were both ethical and accessible.

In those years, every dollar earned came from time traded. Every opportunity required someone else's permission.

That mindset began to shift in the early 1990s when he studied Neuro-Linguistic Programming in New York City. He discovered that his subconscious beliefs, not his external circumstances, were shaping his outcomes. Once he saw this, he began studying belief systems more deeply.

When he shifted his internal beliefs, the results followed. He launched side businesses that, over time, generated more than one million dollars in revenue while still maintaining full-time employment. The strategies were not new. His alignment was.

The turning point was not tactics. It was belief.

Evaluating Your Current Success Beliefs

Success means different things to different people, and your personal definition shapes the direction of your wealth-building journey. For some, success shows up as material abundance, a large home, a luxury car, or a six-figure income. For others, it takes the form of happiness, freedom, and meaningful relationships.

Your beliefs about success are not created in isolation. They are shaped by your upbringing, your environment, and the messages you absorb through media. A family that celebrates financial achievement may raise children who equate success with accumulation. A family that prioritizes joy or service may unintentionally teach that wealth is secondary or unnecessary.

In society and media, success is often framed as something reserved for a select few. These portrayals send subtle signals: only certain people rise to the top, and you must be lucky, connected, or extraordinary to be among them. Over time, those signals can become internalized as silent scripts that influence your financial decisions, often without your awareness.

This raises a deeper question. Do your current beliefs about success match your actual goals and values?

Many coaches and consultants find themselves pursuing income levels that do not reflect their real desires. Some aim too low out of fear. Others aim too high because of external pressure or comparison. In both cases, there is a disconnect between the number and its meaning.

During coaching sessions, clear patterns emerge. Some professionals express satisfaction with minimal income, saying they do not need much or want to avoid stress. In some cases, these are genuine values. In many others, they reflect fear-based beliefs about whether they are truly capable or deserving of more.

On the other hand, some set very high income goals but lack emotional resonance. These goals may come from comparison or ego, not alignment. Without connection, progress stalls and frustration grows.

IDENTIFYING AND HEALING YOUR WEALTH WOUNDS

Money plays a central role in both life and business, and understanding your relationship with it is essential for long-term success. Even individuals who earn substantial incomes may struggle to feel secure or satisfied. That tension often signals deeper wealth wounds.

Wealth wounds are unconscious beliefs about money that are usually formed during childhood or shaped by cultural messages. These beliefs influence financial decisions, pricing, earning potential, and your sense of worth in the marketplace. They can create inner conflict between your values and your goals.

Some of the most financially successful people still live paycheck to paycheck. They may drive luxury cars or own impressive homes, yet privately experience anxiety about bills, debt, or unexpected expenses. Outward success does not heal inner wounds.

Common wealth wounds include beliefs like:

- Money is corrupting or dangerous
- Success must come with sacrifice
- Wanting more is selfish
- You don't deserve abundance
- Spirituality and wealth are in conflict

These beliefs often operate beneath your awareness. They shape your choices without your conscious permission. They make it harder to receive, to raise your rates, to ask for the sale, or to invest in yourself.

Healing begins with reflection. Think back to your earliest memories of money. What did your family say, or not say, about it? Was it a source of stress or secrecy? Was it tied to affection, power, or fear?

In many households, money was either avoided entirely or discussed only in moments of tension. Children absorb these emotional cues even when nothing is said directly. By adulthood, these beliefs can feel like facts.

Schools often reinforced the issue. Many people spent years studying algebra and literature, but never learned how to manage cash flow, evaluate investments, or build financial confidence. And when money was discussed, it was often by teachers who had not experienced financial freedom themselves.

When childhood conditioning and lack of practical tools combine, internal conflict forms. No strategy, no matter how well designed, can override a subconscious belief that whispers, "This is not safe," or "You do not get to have this."

CHALLENGING YOUR INHERITED | MONEY STORIES

Many of the beliefs shaping your financial decisions were not consciously chosen. They were inherited from family, culture, or the limits of early experiences. These inherited money stories often feel like truth, but they are patterns you absorbed, not beliefs you selected.

Most of these stories are rooted in fear, scarcity, or survival thinking. They represent someone else's understanding of safety, not your own.

Common inherited money myths include:

- "Money is the root of all evil"
- "Money doesn't grow on trees"
- "It's hard to make money unless you take advantage of people"
- "You're not smart enough to be wealthy"
- "It's not spiritual to want more"
- "Rich people are greedy or unkind"
- "If I focus on money, I'll lose what really matters"

Even if you do not say these things out loud, they may still be running quietly in the background. And when they are, they create internal conflict that blocks growth.

For example, if you believe that charging premium prices is "taking advantage," you will always underprice yourself, even when you are delivering powerful results. If you have been told that "money does not matter," you may unconsciously push away opportunities that would allow you to earn more.

The first step in rewriting these beliefs is to question their origin. Who told you this? Where did it come from? Was it someone you trust? Did they live the kind of financial life you want for yourself?

When you begin to see these beliefs as inherited rather than created, you open the door to releasing them. You stop defending stories that were never truly yours to begin with.

CREATING NEW WEALTH STORIES

Once you've identified the stories you inherited about money, the next step is to create new ones. Stories that support your growth, align with your values, and reflect who you are now.

This process is not about positive thinking. It is about consciously choosing beliefs that empower you and backing them up with action, evidence, and purpose.

It begins with your motivation. Why do you want financial abundance? What will it allow you to do, give, or create? How will it support the people and causes that matter to you?

Examples of powerful "whys" include:

- Giving back to your community
- Funding scholarships or outreach programs
- Supporting your family or future generations
- Creating time freedom so you can serve more deeply
- Building stability that allows your message to grow

Your "why" must feel personal. If it's borrowed from someone else, it won't hold up during seasons of doubt or challenge.

Once your motivation is clear, you can begin forming new beliefs. Beliefs that align with the future you are building.

Sample belief shifts might include:

- "Money is bad" becomes "Money is a tool I use for good"
- "I don't deserve wealth" is replaced with "I create value and I receive value"
- "Wealth means selling out" turns into "Wealth lets me serve more people and make a bigger impact"

These new stories are reinforced through:

- *Mental rehearsal.* Repeating them out loud, writing them down, speaking them when resistance shows up
- *Surrounding yourself with evidence.* Reading stories of ethical wealth-builders, studying models of service-based abundance
- *Taking aligned action.* Gradually raising your rates, saying yes to bigger opportunities, letting people pay you without guilt or apology

You don't have to shift everything overnight. The process is gradual. But every time you choose a new story and act on it, you create evidence that the new version of you is real.

And over time, those new beliefs become your default.

INSTILLING WEALTH-BUILDING HABITS

Sustainable wealth is not created by a single leap. It is built through small, consistent habits that align your behavior with your beliefs over time. The most financially successful people don't wait for perfect conditions. They act daily in ways that support long-term success.

Wealth-building habits are not about hustle. They are about rhythm, discipline, and clarity of purpose.

Five habits that create lasting financial growth:

1. **Clarify your purpose.**
   Wealth for its own sake rarely inspires lasting change. But wealth connected to a clear purpose—service, freedom, legacy—gives you the energy to show up consistently. What is your reason for building financial stability?

2. **Practice long-term thinking.**
   Wealthy individuals understand delayed gratification. They are willing to trade short-term comforts for long-term rewards. This might mean investing in education, declining a short-term opportunity, or building infrastructure before chasing visibility.

3. **Continue your financial education.**
   The more you learn about money, the more confident you become. Read books. Attend seminars. Listen to podcasts that teach wealth principles. And surround yourself with people who model what is possible.

4. **Balance ambition with gratitude.**
   Wealth is not just about getting more. It's about appreciating what you already have while expanding your capacity to receive. Stay grounded. Stay generous. Stay focused.

5. **Take imperfect action.**
   You do not have to know everything before you begin. Waiting for certainty leads to stagnation. Wealthy people take the next right step—then adjust as they learn. The only way to build is by beginning.

These habits compound over time. Like interest, their impact grows with consistency. You may not see results in a week, but in a year—or five—you will not recognize the person you have become.

THE PATH FORWARD

Transforming your wealth mindset and building lasting financial success is not an overnight process. But it is entirely possible. The journey begins with awareness, moves through belief, and is sustained by aligned, consistent action.

Awareness alone is not enough. You must be willing to act, even when doubt or resistance shows up. The subconscious mind will try to protect old patterns, but persistence will quiet the fear. **Support and repetition create safety. Safety creates movement.**

The coaches and consultants who create financial abundance while staying true to their mission do not treat money as the goal. They see it as a tool for service, stability, and sustainability. They stop treating success and integrity as a trade-off. They understand that the more resourced they are, the more they can help others rise.

Rewriting your wealth story is not only about earning more. It is about receiving in proportion to the value you create. When you begin to believe that your work deserves support, you stop performing for validation and start building from alignment.

Be Paid with Purpose is not about chasing revenue. It is about creating the right relationship between giving and receiving. When you receive with clarity and gratitude, you create space to give more freely.

The next chapter brings everything together. You will see how to integrate each Tenet—*Be Seen, Be Heard, Be Easy to Follow, Be the Solution,* and *Be Paid with Purpose*—into one steady rhythm. This is where your influence becomes visible, measurable, and alive in your daily work.

14

INTEGRATING YOUR INFLUENCE

Donna Kunde

Influence is not something you chase. It's something you practice until it becomes the way you move through the world.

You have walked through each of the Five Tenets of Influence™. You have seen how visibility builds trust, how story deepens connection, and how alignment allows your work to sustain itself. Now it is time to bring these lessons together in a way that feels steady, clear, and true to you.

Integration is not about doing more; it is about allowing what you have learned to take root. The Tenets are not tasks to complete but a way of moving through your work, your message, and your relationships. When they begin to work together, your influence flows with ease rather than effort.

Each one reinforces the others.

Be Seen reminds you to show up.

Be Heard invites you to connect.

Be Easy to Follow keeps your path clear.

Be the Solution keeps your promises aligned with your purpose.

Be Paid with Purpose allows your influence to sustain itself.

This is the moment when clarity becomes rhythm and understanding becomes motion. The small, consistent actions you take now will anchor everything you have built so far and prepare you for what comes next.

THE ALIGNMENT COMPASS

The work ahead is not about adding complexity. It is about bringing your beliefs and your actions into alignment. Use this page as your compass. On one sheet of paper, draw three columns and title them:

New Belief I Am Claiming Now
The Tenet It Strengthens
One Action I Will Take This Week

Then choose one belief, one Tenet, and one small action at a time.

STEP 1: CHOOSE THE BELIEF YOU ARE READY TO STAND IN

Examples:
My voice is allowed to lead.
My work creates real value.
Receiving payment honors the work, the listener, and me.

STEP 2: MATCH THE BELIEF TO THE TENET IT STRENGTHENS

If this belief helps me ...	Then it strengthens ...
Show up visibly	Be Seen
Speak clearly and naturally	Be Heard
Make the next step simple	Be Easy to Follow
Stand confidently in my offer	Be the Solution
Receive payment with openness	Be Paid with Purpose

STEP 3: CHOOSE ONE ACTION YOU CAN COMPLETE IN ONE WEEK

Examples:

Add a clear invitation to the end of your podcast episodes.

Tell a personal story you have avoided.

Raise your price to reflect your value.

Create one simple pathway for how someone can work with you.

Keep it small, real, and doable.

WHY THIS MATTERS

You already have the insight and the message. You already have the Tenets. Now you are choosing to live them.

This is where your podcast becomes a pathway, where your audience begins to follow, and where your business grows from the inside out.

Pause for a moment and look at the progress you have made. You have built a foundation that is steady, clear, and rooted in integrity. The next part of your journey will show how that foundation becomes a business model—how influence moves from inspiration to income through clear, repeatable systems that honor your message and serve your audience.

When you turn the page, you will enter **Part III: Monetization Systems.** Here, you will learn how to align your message, your offers, and your structure so that your work continues to create impact while generating sustainable revenue.

PART IV

MONETIZATION SYSTEMS

By now, your podcast has a clear message and real influence. This section turns that influence into a working business model by walking you through the Podcast Profit System™, the Podcast Profit Playbook™, and the Book Play so your episodes and your book all lead people toward the same transformation. Your show stops guessing and starts following a plan, quietly running a business in the background while you keep serving the people who are ready for more.

15

THE PODCAST PROFIT SYSTEM DECODED

Donna Kunde and James Bryant

Clarity creates movement. A system creates results. The Podcast Profit System™ is where your message becomes a business.

Your podcast is more than a platform for ideas. It is a system for creating change. Once you know who you serve and the problem you solve, the next question becomes clear: How does your podcast guide someone from first contact to meaningful transformation?

The Podcast Profit System™ is where the strategy you built in the Three Worlds of Influence™ becomes action. This is where you start putting your ideas into motion, building structure, designing systems, and creating the flow that turns influence into income. It turns your voice into a business engine built on three Profit Pillars: Build It, Scale It, and Earn It.

You do not have to start over or add more work. This system begins with what you already have. Each 13-week cycle teaches you how to repurpose your message, refine your structure, and create a clear pathway that naturally guides listeners into your business.

THE THREE PROFIT PILLARS

The Podcast Profit System™ rests on three Profit Pillars that support one another. Together, they form a repeatable process that transforms your podcast into a living, growing business. You will learn how to build the foundation that supports your message, scale your systems so they work for you, and earn through aligned offers that serve both you and your audience.

This system is built from real-world experience with podcasters who have achieved measurable results, including six-figure contracts and steady new clients. It provides a working rhythm that supports your growth every 13 weeks.

1. BUILD IT – CREATE YOUR WORKING FOUNDATION

You may feel a twinge of fear at the thought of stepping back from weekly episodes. That reaction is normal. This is not about disappearing. It is about building the structure that allows your voice to last. Your audience does not need more content from you right now. They need clearer pathways to work with you. This 13-week pause is how you create them.

This is the turning point. It is the moment you stop creating new content just to stay visible and start building the business that supports your content.

For 13 weeks, you give yourself permission to step back from constant production. Your audience still hears from you, but through your "Best Of" series or pre-batched episodes. The airwaves stay active while you focus on what most podcasters never make time to do: build the foundation that makes your work sustainable.

This is not stopping. It is shifting. You are moving from creation mode to construction mode, from publishing for validation to designing for profit.

During this cycle, you will:

- Design your first monetization play from the Podcast Profit Playbook™
- Build or refine your funnel so your podcast leads somewhere clear
- Connect your episodes, offers, and emails into one simple listener journey

By the end of this phase, your message no longer depends on your next episode. It stands on its own, supported by systems that serve your audience and your business.

2. SCALE IT - STREAMLINE WHAT WORKS

Once your foundation is in place, you can begin to scale with ease. Scaling is not about doing more. It is about creating flow. You are building systems that carry your message farther without requiring you to work harder.

In this phase, scaling doesn't mean doing more. It means building systems that move your message forward automatically, so your growth feels steady and sustainable. Your podcast episodes, lead magnets, and nurture emails begin to move together as one unified rhythm. Each element reinforces the others and guides listeners toward the next natural step.

Scaling gives you space. You start to see your podcast as part of a larger ecosystem rather than a weekly obligation. The consistency you've built becomes momentum, and that momentum carries your message forward.

During this phase, you will:

- Automate key parts of your funnel so your offers stay active even when you are not
- Repurpose your strongest content into new formats to reach different audiences

- Establish a consistent publishing rhythm supported by clear systems and tools

By the end of this phase, your podcast no longer depends on your constant presence. You have created a structure that allows your message to grow while you focus on serving your audience and refining your offers.

3. Earn It — Monetize with Purpose

Earning is about more than income. It is about alignment. When your podcast, your offers, and your message work together, revenue becomes a natural outcome of service rather than a separate pursuit.

In this phase, you connect your message to your business model. The conversations you start on air naturally lead to offers that feel authentic and helpful. There is no pressure; only clarity about how your audience can take the next step with you.

You also begin to measure what matters: where listeners engage, how they respond, and what inspires them to act. These insights show you where your influence is growing and where to adjust for greater impact.

During this phase, you will:

- Create or refine one aligned offer that reflects your message and values
- Build simple systems for tracking engagement and conversion
- Practice clear, confident invitations that make working with you easy and natural

By the end of this phase, your business begins to sustain itself. Your content attracts the right people, your systems support the relationship, and your offers complete the journey. This is the point where your podcast becomes both purpose-driven and profitable.

THE 13-WEEK RHYTHM

The Podcast Profit System™ runs in repeating 13-week cycles. Each quarter, you focus on one clear goal: building, refining, and launching a single monetization play from the Podcast Profit Playbook™.

This rhythm is what makes the system sustainable. While your podcast continues to air, whether through repurposed or pre-recorded episodes, you stay focused on building the business behind the microphone.

In as little as 13 weeks, you can have a complete, working funnel and your first revenue-generating offer in place.

PUTTING THE SYSTEM INTO MOTION

You now have the structure to move from clarity to profit. The question is not whether the system works. The question is how you will use it.

If you need stability, begin with Build It.

If you are ready for consistency, move to Scale It.

If your structure is ready and you want results, step into Earn It.

Circle the pillar that fits where you are today. Start there. Every pillar supports the next, and every cycle brings greater confidence, visibility, and revenue.

In the next chapter, you will explore The Podcast Profit Playbook™, where you will choose your first monetization play and bring this system to life.

And if another podcaster came to mind as you read, trust that instinct. Sharing this book with them is one of the simplest ways we can expand our collective impact.

Ready to turn your podcast into a business?
Download the Podcast Profit System eBook:
PodcastProfitSystem.com/message-book-resources

16

THE PODCAST PROFIT PLAYBOOK

The business model, not just the show.
Donna Kunde and James Bryant

You don't need massive download numbers or corporate sponsors to profit from your podcast. You need a clear intention, a focused message, and a plan for how your show supports your business.

For many podcasters, the common belief is that success comes from large audiences, ad networks, and brand partnerships. This creates pressure to grow numbers rather than strengthening the value already present in the message and the audience you have now.

The truth is more practical and more encouraging.

Most podcasters do not need millions of listeners. They need alignment between what they talk about, who they talk to, and how they invite those listeners to take the next step.

A podcast can be a hobby. It can also be a business model.

The difference is whether you have a way to turn your message into movement.

This is where the Podcast Profit Playbook™ comes in.

The Playbook outlines nine reliable monetization paths. You do not need all nine. You only need one to begin. Each play works because it connects your expertise to the transformation your listeners are already seeking.

When you stop trying to entertain everyone and start serving someone, your podcast shifts from something people listen to into something people act on.

Old models have shaped the beliefs around podcast monetization. It is time to consider a different approach.

BREAKING FREE FROM THE VANITY METRICS TRAP

For years, conventional wisdom in podcasting seemed fixed. Launch your show, chase more downloads, secure corporate sponsors, and measure success by audience size. The industry rewarded reach instead of depth. It encouraged constant promotion rather than strengthening the message.

This approach pushes many podcasters into a cycle of pressure and comparison. It turns mission-driven creators into hesitant marketers seeking external validation. The more they chase numbers, the further they drift from the purpose that inspired their voice.

The truth is that the traditional advertising model is exhausting. It works only when you already have a massive audience or are willing to shape your content around sponsor demands. Most podcasters end up stuck, focused on downloads while struggling to cover even basic production costs.

But what if everything you've been told about podcast monetization is wrong?

Sustainable profit does not come from ads, sponsorships, or audience size alone. It comes from treating your podcast as a business asset. Your show becomes a place to demonstrate your expertise, build trust, and guide listeners toward the transformation they are already seeking.

When you make this shift, the central question changes.

You stop asking:

What will get me more listeners?

And you begin asking:

What transformation are my current listeners seeking, and how can I help them take the next step?

This is the shift that turns a podcast from a hobby into a business model.

THE NINE PLAY FRAMEWORK

The Podcast Profit Playbook provides nine reliable ways to generate revenue from your show. You do not need all nine to begin. You only need one clear direction. One play creates movement. Trying to do everything at once creates overwhelm and stalls progress.

The Playbook begins with a simple question:

Do you already have something to sell?

If you already have an offer such as a coaching program, consulting package, course, membership, or service, you begin with a play that uses your podcast as a trust-building path into that offer.

If you do not yet have something to sell, you begin with a play that helps you create your first sellable asset.

Each podcaster naturally aligns with a play that reflects how they already serve and create transformation. The play you choose reflects the way you already help people.

Across all nine plays, one stands out as foundational:

The Book Play

A book gives your voice permanence and credibility. It turns your spoken ideas into something tangible that can be shared, referenced, and returned to over time. As a podcaster, you already possess most of the material you need. You have been speaking your book into existence one episode at a time.

You are not starting from zero.

You are starting from 80 percent complete.

STARTING WITH WHAT YOU ALREADY HAVE

Your episodes already contain your stories, your insights, and your frameworks. You have already been teaching. You have already been guiding. The content is there.

Your podcast is already a library of what you know.

Now you choose which doorway to open first.

LEVERAGING EXISTING CONTENT

- *Podcast to Course*: Turn a set of themed episodes into a guided learning experience. The value is in the structure.
- *Membership or Community*: If your listeners want ongoing support, create a place to grow together.

HIGH VALUE REVENUE STREAMS

- *Dream Client Conversations*: Build trust through meaningful dialogue.
- *Workshops or Corporate Training*: Package your frameworks into outcomes organizations want.
- *Premium Offers*: Deliver focused transformation at a deeper level.

SCALING THROUGH COLLABORATION

- *Joint Ventures*: Grow together with aligned partners.
- *Live Events and Workshops*: Create shared learning moments.
- *Affiliate and Referral Networks*: Let others help your message spread.

These plays expand your reach without increasing your workload.

HOW YOUR PLAY FITS INSIDE THE SYSTEM

In the previous chapter, you learned how the Podcast Profit System™ turns your message into a path that listeners can follow. The Playbook is where you decide how you will guide that transformation.

Your Play is the way you help people. The format is not the point. The transformation is the point.

Inside the Podcast Profit System™, your Play becomes the center of your business. Your podcast becomes the way your audience enters your world, learns from you, and chooses whether to take the next step.

The system runs in repeating cycles:

Phase 1: Build the Foundation

Clarify the transformation your Play offers and create one clear invitation.

Phase 2: Be Heard with Authority

Organize your strongest past episodes into a Signature Season that leads somewhere on purpose.

Phase 3: Monetize with Purpose

Host one meaningful connection event and extend an invitation to deeper work.

Phase 4: Make It Easy to Say Yes

Your message and your episodes now reinforce each other. Your podcast continues working even when you are not recording.

Your Play does not sit outside the system; it powers the system. You do not need all nine Plays. You only need one to begin. And one Play strengthens them all.

The Book Play.

Your book is already spoken. Your message is already developed. Your voice already carries your authority. You are eighty percent finished. Now we complete the final twenty percent.

Turn the page.

With this handy resource, you'll have everything you need to turn your podcast into a business. Go here for the Podcast Profit Playbook™:

PodcastProfitSystem.com/message-book-resources.

And if another podcaster came to mind as you read, trust that instinct. Sharing this book with them is one of the simplest ways we can expand our collective impact.

17

THE BOOK PLAY
(YOUR 80% ADVANTAGE)

By Sheila Slick, Founder of PodToBook.ai

You have already done the hardest part. You showed up. You recorded. You taught. You told stories. Your book is not something you start now. Your book is something you reveal from the work you have already done.

You now have a clear path for how your podcast can support your business. You also saw nine different ways to turn your message into revenue. The play you choose shapes the next step you will take.

Podcasters often begin with the Book Play because it offers a simple starting point. Your ideas are already spoken. Your stories are already recorded. Your voice is already familiar to your audience. The work now is to give those ideas a form they can hold, share, and return to.

Most creators feel pressure to begin from scratch. They try to write a book from a blank page, build a course before there is demand, or design a full coaching program without momentum. It is understandable that this feels overwhelming.

Here is the easier path. If you have a podcast, you have already done most of the work. Your episodes already contain your message, your voice, your lived expertise, and your perspective. **What if you could turn those recorded conversations into a first book draft in about two hours?** What if your podcast and your book worked together to open doors, build authority, and welcome the right people into your world?

This is not a theory. This is the story of someone who solved this exact problem and, in doing so, created a tool that has now helped thousands of podcasters take the next step.

THE GENESIS OF INNOVATION

Sheila Slick did not set out to build a software platform. She was simply trying to solve a problem she kept running into as a podcaster. On her show, *Milestone Moments in Business and Leadership*, she recorded powerful conversations filled with ideas, frameworks, and lessons that deserved to live beyond audio. But they remained stored and unused.

"I have all of these great episodes, and they are just sitting there," Sheila says. "As a creator, you have to ask how to repurpose what you already have. Not everyone listens to podcasts. Some people prefer to read."

The problem wasn't content. The problem was format.

Sheila had been an entrepreneur most of her life: jeweler, software developer, business consultant. Each role trained her to notice inefficiencies and improve systems. So when AI tools became more accessible, she began exploring ways to simplify her workflow. Transcription tools could capture the words, but the cleanup, organization, and rewriting still took hours. Every episode came out differently. The inconsistency was the real barrier.

Most people would have stopped there. Sheila didn't. She needed a solution, so she decided to build one.

Years earlier, while living overseas with three young children and helping run a family business, she taught herself to code at age thirty-six, not because she wanted to become a developer, but because she saw that technology was the future. "Who is going to teach my kids this?" she remembers thinking. "This is something they need." That decision shaped her approach to everything that followed: learn early, experiment, and build what is needed rather than wait for someone else to solve the problem.

"The internet is a window to the world," she says. "And this was before AI."

So when the time came, she didn't see PodToBook.ai as a big, intimidating idea. She saw it as the next practical solution to a familiar problem—a way to give recorded conversations a second life on the page.

FROM CONCEPT TO REALITY

The idea for PodToBook.ai began after a podcast interview. When the recording ended, Sheila and her guest kept talking. He asked if she had ever tried working with AI in her coding.

"I told him I was afraid of it," Sheila says. "Everything about it seemed intricate and overwhelming."

He did not try to persuade her. He simply said, "Take one of your apps and let your imagination go."

She sat with that. Instead of trying to build something complex, she focused on solving her own problem. She wanted a way to take the conversations she had already recorded and turn them into writing she could actually use.

"Why not focus it on something I need?" she thought. "If it works for me, then I will know the quality is good before anyone else sees it."

She tested every feature on her own content. She refined the tool until the output felt seamless.

"I am a perfectionist in many ways," Sheila says. "Before I share anything, I need to know it works well enough that I would use it myself."

That commitment shaped the tool. PodToBook.ai was not built to impress. It was built to solve a real problem faced by real creators.

Your book is already in your voice. It is already spoken. It is already recorded. The work now is simply bringing it to the page.

PodToBook.ai began with one question:

What if the book has already been written, and we just need a way to see it?

What if the content you already recorded could become your book?

THE SIMPLICITY REVOLUTION

One of the most important parts of PodToBook.ai is how simple it is to use. Sheila built it so that anyone with recorded audio can turn that audio into written material without needing special training or technical skill.

"What I set out to do was keep the app simple," Sheila says. "In three steps you share your audio, select a few episodes, and press the 'Generate Book' button. Then you sit back and wait. It takes about two hours for the system to process the audio and turn it into a manuscript."

The process works like this:

- Import your podcast feed.
- Enter your podcast's RSS link (or upload audio files to a free RSS Builder) so the system can access your episodes in one place.
- Choose the episodes you want to include.
- Most people select episodes that share a theme so the book feels focused and clear.
- Click Generate Book.
- The system processes the audio and creates a written draft. It will arrive in your email when it is ready.

Under the surface, the platform is doing more than transcription. It organizes the flow of ideas, shapes the conversation into readable form, and preserves tone and intent. It does not simply paste text together. It creates narrative from spoken language.

We used PodToBook.ai to create the early draft of this book. We gathered working-session recordings, podcast episodes, and training conversations. Then we created a custom RSS feed to pull them into one place. PodToBook.ai processed the audio and produced a manuscript that became the foundation of what you are reading now.

"It is proof of concept," Sheila says. "If it can take content from multiple voices and different formats and still create something usable, it can work for anyone who has recorded conversation."

The value is not just speed. It is relief—from months of transcription work, from the overwhelming shift between speaking and writing, from watching valuable content sit unused because the path to publication is so time-consuming.

BEYOND PODCASTS

PodToBook.ai was first created for podcasters, but people quickly began using it in ways Sheila did not expect. The idea is simple: any meaningful spoken conversation can be turned into written content.

"One of my clients said this is a pitch book," Sheila explains. Instead of creating a full book from many episodes, this client selected a single conversation, turned it into a short PDF, and shared it with podcast guests and potential clients. It became a polished leave-behind that clearly communicated their expertise.

Workshops, roundtable discussions, coaching calls, and interviews can all be transformed into resources people can revisit and share. The spoken word does not have to disappear once the conversation ends.

If you record it, you can repurpose it.

THE CONTENT CREATOR'S ADVANTAGE

Most podcasters have already created more value than they realize. Years of episodes, interviews, and trainings sit stored in audio form. The ideas are strong, but they are locked in a format that only a listener who finds the episode can access.

Turning that audio into written content by hand is slow. You would need to transcribe it, clean it up, organize the ideas, and rewrite it into a readable flow. That is why most podcasters never do it, even when the material is good.

PodToBook.ai removes that barrier. One episode can become a chapter. A themed series can become a guide. A training session can become a workbook.

Your archive is not old content. It is stored value.

When you unlock it, you are not starting from zero. You are building from work you have already done.

QUALITY CONTROL IN THE AGE OF AI

PodToBook.ai does much of the heavy lifting, but the draft you receive is a starting point, not a finished book.

"I always tell people, this is a first draft," Sheila says. "It is not something you copy and upload straight into Amazon. The human in the loop is essential. You need to proofread, verify names and details, and make it truly your own."

The platform handles transcription, organization, and flow. It turns spoken ideas into written form. But only you can add the personal touches that make the book sound like you: your stories, your examples, your emphasis.

The tool removes the part that stops most people from ever writing at all. It clears the path.

Your voice leads it the rest of the way.

THE TWO-HOUR ADVANTAGE

The most powerful part of PodToBook.ai is the time it returns to the creator. Sheila did not set out to replace the author. She removed the part of the process that stops most people before they ever begin.

In about two hours, you receive a clear first draft of your book. Not a transcript. Not stitched-together quotes. A manuscript with structure, flow, and your voice still present.

Most people think writing a book means starting from a blank page. But if you have been podcasting, speaking, teaching, or coaching, you have already spoken the ideas. The stories are recorded. The message is already alive.

PodToBook.ai simply brings the book forward from what already exists.

This is your eighty percent advantage. You are not starting from zero. You are building from momentum. Your podcast is the raw material. The first draft of your book may already be recorded.

It is just waiting to be revealed.

And once your draft is in hand, the next step is bringing it to life.

In the following chapter, publishing expert Chris O'Byrne will walk you through how to turn your manuscript into a professional book that reflects your voice, builds your authority, and helps the right readers find you.

18

SELF-PUBLISHING THAT SELLS

By Chris O'Byrne, Founder of Jetlaunch Publishing

Your book should be your best marketing tool, your best salesperson, and your relationship builder. It should go places you can't go, have conversations you can't have, and keep working long after you close your laptop.

Chris O'Byrne sits in his home office, adjusting his camera before another call begins. A framed photo of his daughter sits on the table next to him. She is wearing a ballet costume and smiling. The photo is not a decoration, however; it's his reminder of why the work matters.

"There are two reasons I do this," Chris says. "One is for the author who has something important to say. I want them to have a real chance at reaching people and changing someone's life. The other reason is for her. I want her to be proud of me. I want her to know her dad helped people in a real way."

His voice is steady. There is no rush in how he speaks. He has been teaching authors for almost two decades, and the pace reflects a quiet confidence.

THE REALITY OF PUBLISHING TODAY

More than one million new books are published every year. Millions more are already available. Most will never be seen or read. Not because they're bad, but because no one knows they exist.

Chris calls this *the crowded room*. Picture yourself in a huge room with one million other people. Everyone is waving a book and hoping someone notices. If your launch plan is simply "list the book on Amazon," you become one of those people waving in that crowd and hoping for luck. Luck is not a plan.

This is where many authors begin to feel lost. They start searching online for marketing shortcuts, and he internet is full of people promising fast success. They promise thousands of sales or bestseller status in a weekend. Chris has seen these promises for years.

"Most of the people selling those systems are not experts in selling books," he says. "They are experts in selling the idea of success. They make their money on the promise, not the result."

YOUR BOOK HAS A JOB

A book is not meant to sit on a shelf; it should work hard for you. It should speak for you when you're not in the room. It should show your way of thinking. It should introduce your method or process. It should help someone really understand what it would be like to work with you.

Your book is not only a story or a message. It is a tool for connection.

When a book is built with intention, it does four things:

- Shows that you understand your reader
- Explains the problem clearly
- Offers a first step that creates a real result
- Invites the reader to continue learning with you

These steps work whether the book is instructional, inspirational, or story-driven. The form doesn't matter; the structure of the connection does.

WHY SELF-PUBLISHING GIVES YOU CONTROL

Many authors believe traditional publishing is the "real" route. Chris explains a different perspective. In traditional publishing, the author loses control of their own book. The publisher can edit language, remove parts, or not allow direct calls-to-action. This is because it's no longer your book; it belongs to your publisher. This severely limits how the book can support your business.

"If your goal is to make an impact and build relationships, you need the right to speak directly to your reader," Chris says. "You need the freedom to guide them to the next step. Self-publishing allows that."

Self-publishing also allows updates. As your message grows, so can your book. You can revise examples, add new tools, and improve clarity over time. The book becomes a living part of your business, not a frozen artifact from your past. You can decide to make a change on Monday and have your updated book available to purchase by Friday.

WRITING FOR CONNECTION, NOT PERFORMANCE

There are three core principles Chris teaches every author:

1. Describe the reader's problem clearly
2. Speak to what the reader is actually experiencing. Use real language, not general statements. Meet the reader in the reality of what they feel, not only what they think.
3. Offer a quick win
4. Give the reader something they can do within a week that leads to a noticeable shift. Big transformation takes time. Trust grows when progress happens early.

5. Make the next step simple
6. The invitation should feel natural. No pressure. No pitch. Just a clear doorway for the reader who is ready to continue. This may be a worksheet, a recorded lesson, or a short guide that helps them deepen what they have begun.

The goal is not to sell but to support. When the reader feels supported, the relationship continues on its own.

When the Book Begins Working for You

Your book becomes a relationship builder. It creates understanding before you meet. It shows how you think and what matters to you. It introduces the reader to your voice and your approach. By the time someone reaches out, they already know who you are. The conversation starts at a deeper level.

This is how a book becomes part of a business, not a project that ends after publication.

Your book is now a working part of your business. It will carry your message into new conversations and new relationships. Before you publish, there is one more step. You must protect your work. Your ideas, your frameworks, and your voice are part of your business. They need to be secured so no one else can claim what you have created.

In the next chapter, you will learn how to protect your intellectual property and safeguard the foundation you are now building.

PART V

FUTURE-PROOF YOUR INFLUENCE

This is where you protect what you have built and the life it is meant to support. These chapters help you claim and steward your brand through trademarks, then design a way of working where success at the microphone does not cost you your health, your relationships, or your purpose. By the end, you will see your message not only as a business asset but as a lifelong calling you can grow, guard, and enjoy.

19

NAME IT. USE IT. KEEP IT.

By Wayne Carroll, Founder of Inspired Idea Solutions®
Law Firm

You can actually lose your trademark rights if you
don't enforce them. The same goes for renewals.
You don't want to wait until it is too late to renew
your trademarks or to take action when
someone else is using them.

In Chapter 10, we explored what happens when a podcast becomes more than just a podcast. That is when your ideas begin to generate income. But building a profitable platform is not only about what you create. It is also about what you protect.

That is where Wayne Carroll comes in.

Wayne has decades of experience helping entrepreneurs and creators guard their most valuable business assets: their ideas, their brands, and their voice. As a patent attorney and founder of Inspired Idea Solutions, he has seen the damage that happens when people wait too long to claim what is already theirs. His work bridges the gap between creativity and legal strategy. He gives purpose-driven entrepreneurs the tools to build lasting influence without losing control of the business they are working so hard to grow.

In this chapter, Wayne shares what every podcaster and content creator needs to understand about trademarks, protection, and ownership.

Before we move into the next stage of building, we pause to look at something most business owners overlook.

Your message, your story, your programs, and your podcast all live inside a name and a brand. A brand is not just a label. It is the container for your reputation, your credibility, and the trust you earn over time. This earned trust is called goodwill, and it is one of the most valuable parts of your business.

You have worked hard to build that trust. You have shown up, created value, shared your ideas, and guided others. But a message without protection is vulnerable. A brand without clarity is exposed. Influence without ownership can be taken by someone who simply moves faster, files earlier, or uses the system more deliberately.

Your brand is property, just like a car or a house, you can rent, buy, and sell brands (usually when selling the entire business). A title says who owns a car, and a deed says who owns a house. The owner has the right to say who can and who cannot use the property.

For a brand, trademark law says who the owner is, and who gets to tell others they can and cannot use the brand. A registered trademark is like the title to a car. When your brand has a registered trademark, the government says you own the trademark.

THE BIGGEST PROBLEM IN THE UNIVERSE

A Joint Venture is Created: In 2012, Dax and George began working together to produce a podcast, *The Biggest Problem in the Universe*. The first episode was published in 2014, and the podcast continued until 2016, building the brand and a following. The joint venture was an oral agreement, not in writing, and they shared the profits 50/50.

Disagreements Arose: Dax and George could not agree on continuing to produce episodes, splitting the profits, or how to move forward with the joint venture. Tensions rose, and the joint venture began to fall apart while they continued marketing the podcast. The business relationship was severed in 2016.

George Files a Trademark and a Lawsuit: In 2017, things went from bad to worse. George, on his own, without Dax, filed for the trademark *The Biggest Problem in the Universe*. George also filed a harassment lawsuit against Dax.

Dax Files a Trademark Lawsuit: Then Dax filed a lawsuit to stop George from getting the trademark. The biggest question was who owned the trademark rights. The court determined that the joint venture owned the rights, so George could not get trademark rights without Dax. The lawsuit took about 10 months and was likely very costly for both Dax and George. Ultimately, in April of 2018, the court stopped George's trademark application and Dax won the case.

Dax Gets the Trademark: A few years later, in 2021, Dax filed a new trademark application and was granted a federally registered trademark for *The Biggest Problem in the Universe* for podcasts.

Conclusion: With better planning, this costly trademark battle could have been avoided. This was a messy business divorce, and the brand was the child caught in the middle. Neither party originally put in place proper planning for the brand assets they were creating, including how they would be owned and protected.

Solution: Protecting your brand is both strategic and personal. The earlier you start planning, the better. Working with a trademark attorney on a legal strategy will give your brand room to grow. Trademark strategy is based on what your business will become, not only what it is today.

As your podcast grows, so does the value of the brand behind it, and a trademark protects that brand and name. Listeners begin to connect the name with your voice, your ideas, and the help you provide. This is where trademarks become part of building a real business. A trademark protects the path your listeners follow into your world. It keeps your name from being used by others and protects the trust you are working so hard to earn. You do not need to protect everything. You only need to protect the parts of your message that support your business and the future you are building.

And this is where we turn to the practical work of naming, using, and keeping your identity in the marketplace.

GOOD STRATEGY REQUIRES GOOD INFORMATION

One of the first steps in a trademark strategy is to research whether the brand and the trademark that represents it are available without infringing the rights of others.

This research is recommended even if you have already launched and built goodwill around your name. Imagine you are living in a home and someone arrives to tell you that you do not own the home and must move out right away. This is what can happen if you build a brand without checking that the name is available. The owner of the brand can force you to stop using the name. You will have to start over.

Working with a professional to determine availability before taking action is the best strategy. There are tools to do your own preliminary searches, but the nuances of trademark law can give you a different result than you expect.

BADASS LEADER vs. BADASS CEO

Planning Ahead: Edna and Malcom MacLean planned to launch a podcast called *Badass CEO*. They did not see any trademarks registered for this exact name, so they filed a trademark application early, before they used it.

Approval from the Trademark Office: After overcoming some hurdles, the MacLeans received approval from the Trademark Office.

Trademark Opposed: After the trademark office approves a trademark, anyone outside the office may oppose its registration. A company with a DBA and trademarks for *Badass Leader* filed an opposition, a type of lawsuit, to stop the trademark application.

Negotiations: The MacLeans and *Badass Leader* reached an agreement, allowing the MacLeans' application to move forward.

Conclusion: The MacLeans were fortunate to reach an agreement. Not all stories end this way. Many times, a trademark that appears to be available by doing a search in the trademark office is actually too close to someone's existing trademark. Many companies run searches weekly or monthly to identify trademark applications they consider too close to their own. Even if the Trademark Office approves the trademark, other companies, with or without prior trademark registrations, can oppose the application and prevent it from becoming a registered trademark.

Solution: To avoid this result, a professional can conduct thorough research to assess the risk of rejection based on prior-filed trademarks and other companies opposing the trademark application. Sometimes a strategy can be explored before filing the trademark to greatly improve the chances of success.

Good research looks not only at the United States Trademark Office but also at companies that may have earlier use of the name on similar goods or services. Even after your trademark is registered, a company with prior use of the trademark can cancel your trademark in a lawsuit. You do not want to obtain a trademark only to have it canceled later.

HOW TO USE YOUR TRADEMARK CORRECTLY

Trademark rights are strengthened when the trademark is used correctly. They weaken when the mark becomes generic or unclear. There are three key guidelines for proper trademark use:

1. **Use your trademark as an adjective.**
   A trademark identifies the source. It should modify a noun.

   For example: "ABC brand coaching program" instead of "ABC is the program."

2. **Make the trademark stand out.**
   Use capital letters or a consistent style so readers know it is a brand name.

3. **Use the correct symbol.**
   Use the TM symbol before your mark is registered.

Use the R in a circle only after the registration certificate is issued.

Using the Circle R too early is illegal and can result in the loss of rights. It is safer to use TM until registration is complete. Decide which names and terms will belong only to your business, and begin marking them with TM.

MAINTAINING YOUR RIGHTS OVER TIME

Registering a trademark is not the finish line. It is the beginning of ongoing stewardship. Once your mark is in use, you must monitor how it appears in the marketplace. If another business begins using a confusingly similar name, you may need to address it. Trademark rights weaken when they are not actively protected.

EVA'S BRIDAL

A Family Run Business: Eva's Bridal was a growing family-run business with several locations in Chicago, owned by the Zahr family. Different family members owned different locations. As the brand continued to grow, the family licensed the trademark to Halanick Enterprises, Inc., and the Zahr family collected royalties for the use of the Eva's Bridal brand.

Lack of Control: Unfortunately, the license was not properly set up to give the family control over how the trademark was used and what could and could not be done with the brand. Trademark law requires that you control the trademark so that consumers get an experience controlled by the same company whenever they interact with the brand.

No More Royalties: Halanick Enterprises, Inc. decided to stop paying royalties, and the Zahr family sued for trademark infringement. After examining the nature of the agreements between the parties, the court decided that Eva's Bridal was not an enforceable trademark because it did not have control of the experience of consumers when they interacted with the trademark.

Conclusion: If you don't control the use of your trademark, you can lose your rights to stop others from using your trademark. In this case, it was because Zahr licensed the trademark without sufficient controls, but this also happens with trademark owners who allow competitors to infringe their trademarks for years without taking any steps to control the use of the brand.

Solution: Control and Enforcement do not always require constant confrontation. It means staying aware of how your brand is represented and how others in your industry may be using similar branding. You can monitor how others are using your brand through internal systems and procedures, and by hiring experts to set up sound monitoring systems. Some companies post pages on their websites about their trademark rights, and others have even run full-page ads in newspapers and magazines to raise awareness of their brand and trademark rights.

Trademarks Can Last Forever, If Maintained: Renewals are also part of maintaining your rights. Trademark owners in the United States must file proof of continued use between the fifth and sixth year after registration, and again between every ninth and tenth year. Missing these deadlines can result in your registration being cancelled, even if you are still using the brand.

It is helpful to keep simple records of how your mark appears in marketing, sales pages, packaging, or digital products. These records support renewal filings and show that your mark is still active in commerce.

Monitoring and renewal are not complicated. They are steady habits. Just as you care for your message, your audience, and your systems, you care for your trademark in small, consistent ways. This is how your brand remains strong over time.

The goal is not to become an expert in trademark law. The goal is to maintain control over your message as it grows. For many podcasters, this begins with protecting the show's name. As you build your first offer or course, you may choose to protect the name of your program or your signature method. These steps help your business grow with confidence because you know your brand belongs to you.

Why This Matters to Your Podcast and Your Offer

Your brand name is the identity your audience learns to trust. It is tied to your reputation and your message. As your podcast grows and your offers gain traction, the name becomes even more important. This is when others may try to use something similar. If you have not protected your trademark, it becomes difficult to prevent market confusion.

Many podcasters discover too late that someone else has filed a trademark application for their show name after it has grown. When that happens, the creator must change the name, lose momentum, and rebuild the trust they already earned.

Trademark protection gives you peace of mind. It gives you ownership. It helps you protect what you are building.

You have worked to create influence, value, and trust. Your brand deserves the same care you bring to your audience and your work. Decide whether working with a trademark attorney to develop and carry out a trademark strategy is right for your business.

Now that you know how to protect the business on the outside, we will turn our attention to something equally important. You.

The systems you build, the audience you serve, and the success you create are all connected to your ability to remain grounded and whole. A business can grow only as strong as the person leading it.

So before we move forward, we pause and ask a different question:

What are you building all of this for?

20

WIN AT WORK AND WIN AT HOME

By Dr. James Bryant, Host of Engineer Your Success Podcast

Success is not just what you build in the world. It is the life you are able to live while you build it. Winning at work and winning at home is not a tradeoff. It is something you design on purpose, with clarity, intention, and love.

You have built something meaningful. You have learned how to shape your message, build your brand, and protect the intellectual property that supports your work. But before you take the next step, pause and ask yourself one question:

What are you building all this for?

FROM BUILDING TO BECOMING

I have spent most of my life building things. I built projects, systems, businesses, and even habits of achievement. Like many of you, I believed that if I worked hard enough and stayed committed, everything in life would eventually balance out.

It did not.

I learned that the hard way early in my career. On the same day I was offered a dream job in Washington, D.C., my wife told me we were expecting our first child. I took the job anyway. I believed I could have both.

On paper, I was winning. But in real life, I was exhausted and disconnected from the people who mattered most.

That tension forced me to stop and ask three questions that changed my life:

- Do you want to win at work?
- Do you want to win at home?
- Are you?

If your answer to the third question feels uncertain, you are not alone. I have been there too.

The way forward is not choosing work or family. It is learning to integrate the two.

THE REAL ASSET

You have done the work to protect your business. You have guarded your brand, your message, and your intellectual property. But there is something even more valuable to protect: your peace, your people, and your purpose.

When my second son was born prematurely, I drove hours each day while he fought for his life in the NICU. That season stripped away every illusion of control. It reminded me that success is not only about what we build. It is about who and what we are building for.

Your intellectual property is an asset. But your relationships and your well-being are irreplaceable. The systems you have created are tools. The life those systems support is what matters most.

WINNING AT WORK *AND* AT HOME

For years, I believed balance meant splitting myself between the two worlds. I tried to squeeze family time around endless tasks and deadlines. Over time, I realized that work and home are not competing priorities. When aligned, they strengthen each other.

When I started *Engineer Your Success*, it was not only about career growth. It was about designing a life where both work and home could thrive. I call this *Dynamic Balance*. It is the ability to adjust your rhythm as life changes, without losing yourself.

People who learn to win in both places tend to do a few things well:

- They know what matters most.
- They build routines that support their values.
- They stay connected to the people they love.
- They manage energy, not just time.
- They practice celebration, because joy must be claimed, not postponed.

This is not a checklist. It is a way of living.

STEWARDSHIP OVER OWNERSHIP

You have learned how to protect your brand. But true protection goes beyond paperwork and legal claims. It is about stewardship.

You are not only the creator of your business. You are the caretaker of the life it supports.

When I turned down a major promotion that would have required me to live in D.C. full-time, it was not because I lacked ambition. It was because I finally had clarity. My employer later offered me the same role with flexibility. That moment taught me a simple truth:

When your values lead, opportunities realign to meet you.

Your message and your mission are extensions of who you are. Protecting both means designing a life where you can live your message, not just speak it.

DESIGNING A LIFE THAT CAN HOLD YOUR SUCCESS

The best engineers design systems that bend without breaking. They expect stress and change. They build flexibility and recovery into the structure.

Your life works the same way. You cannot control every challenge. But you can choose how you prepare, how you support yourself, and how you return to what matters.

Before you move forward, take a moment to reflect:

- What are you optimizing your life and business for?
- Who benefits most when you are fully present?
- What boundaries or practices need strengthening right now?
- How will you measure alignment, not just achievement?

Your answers to these questions will guide what comes next.

A FINAL WORD

You have shaped your message. You have built your business. You have learned how to protect what you have created.

Now it is time to protect why you created it.

You can build a life that is integrated, sustainable, and meaningful. One where your work supports your home. One where your voice supports your purpose. One where success does not cost you yourself.

I have walked this road. I continue to walk it every day. I can tell you this with full confidence:

It is worth it.

I am Dr. James Bryant, your Coach in Your Corner.

Let us keep building what is worth protecting.

As you just heard, building a business is not only about the systems or strategies. It is about building a life that can hold the weight of your mission. In the final chapter, we will bring everything together so you can move forward with clarity, purpose, and momentum.

THE BEGINNING OF YOUR
NEXT CHAPTER

Everything that I build is an answer to how do I...?
how do I...? how do I...? Just because you're starting at zero in
our space doesn't mean that you have no knowledge to share.
You have a wealth of knowledge to share that people are
searching for right now.

Thank you for coming this far. You stayed with the work, you stayed with the questions, and you stayed with the parts of your message that matter most. My hope is that this book has helped you see what is already possible when your voice, your experience, and your purpose come together. As we close, I want to leave you with one more truth as you move forward.

The traditional wisdom about podcast monetization is flawed. You do not need millions of downloads. You do not need sponsors. You do not need to wait until you "build an audience" before your podcast can earn revenue.

The podcasters who succeed understand something different.

Quality matters more than quantity.

The system you just learned was built from real people asking real questions in real time. When the world shut down in 2020, the question was simple.

How do I keep serving my audience when everything is changing?

What began as radio programming to help coaches and experts stay connected became something more. Week after week, podcasters kept asking the same question.

How do I turn my podcast into a business?

The answer became what you now know as the Podcast Profit System. A system refined across more than fifteen thousand episodes, in fourteen countries, shaped by what works in real implementation rather than speculation.

THE THREE PILLARS

You have already seen how they work. They have guided you toward clarity, connection, and structure, and now they provide the support you need to turn your message into a business.

BUILD IT.

Being easy to follow matters. Your audience should always know the next step. A podcast without a pathway is just content. A podcast with a pathway is a business.

SELL IT.

Your transcripts are intellectual property. Your conversations already contain your methods, frameworks, stories, and offers. You are not starting from scratch. You are shaping what you have already created.

SCALE IT.

Your business should support your life, not consume it. Growth happens through systems and relationships, not endless output or algorithm chasing.

THE REAL SHIFT

Podcast monetization is not about reaching everyone. It is about going deeper with the people who are already listening.

This work centers on conversation, clarity, and community. It invites people not just to consume your message, but to participate in it.

People are not looking for more content.

They are looking for a place to belong while they create change in their lives.

This is where the Podcast Profit Lab comes in.

It gives you a place to implement, not just learn.

A place to be supported, not just inspired.

A place to build the offer your audience has already been asking for.

You do not have to build this alone.

And you do not have to figure it out from scratch.

If another podcaster came to mind as you read, trust that instinct. Sharing this book with them is one of the simplest ways we can expand our collective impact.

You already have your message.

You already have your experience.

You already have people who are listening.

Now you simply build the pathway that leads them forward.

And you do not have to take that step by yourself.

Your Friend on the Journey,
Donna

Let's connect!

Ready to implement what you've learned?

Join the Podcast Profit Lab™ and turn your message into momentum: PodcastProfitSystem.com.

ABOUT THE AUTHORS

Donna Kunde
Founder of the Podcast Profit System™

Donna Kunde is the founder of the Podcast Profit System™ and the creator of all the intellectual property in this book. She is an internationally bestselling author, global radio host, and Podcast Profit Strategist who has helped produce more than 15,000 podcast episodes with over 1.5 million downloads.

Through her work, Donna helps podcasters, authors, and entrepreneurs turn their message into a business that makes a difference. Her programs include Business Podcasting Made Easy™, Podcast Profit Playbook™, and the Influence Radio™ Network. Each one reflects her belief that success comes from real systems, real support, and real results.

Learn more at podcastprofitsystem.com.

Dr. James Bryant

Dr. James Bryant, Ph.D., P.E., is the founder of *Engineer Your Success*, an executive coaching and consulting firm helping engineering and technical leaders "win at work and at home." A professional engineer turned executive coach, Dr. Bryant integrates his technical background with over two decades of leadership experience to help professionals and entrepreneurs design systems for sustainable success.

Through his coaching practice, public speaking, and the *Engineer Your Success Podcast*, he equips leaders to align their faith, family, and work so they can thrive without compromise.

Dr. Bryant lives in Virginia with his wife and sons, where he continues to model the message he teaches: success isn't just what you build; it's who you become along the way.

Sheila Slick

Sheila Slick, MS, is the Founder and President of *Five Milestones LLC* and *PodToBook.ai*, where she supports experts, solopreneurs, and service-based entrepreneurs in amplifying their authority, streamlining their systems, and scaling their impact online.

A technology entrepreneur who has received NASA Space Apps Global Recognitions (2013, 2016) for her educational apps, Sheila is recognized as a Female Pioneer in Technology in Latin America. She has co-founded four businesses across multiple countries and brings over 25 years of leadership experience to her work.

As Past Chair of SCORE Volusia Flagler County, Sheila led a volunteer team that mentored over 720 small business owners annually during her tenure. She holds a Master of Science in Leadership from Embry-Riddle Aeronautical University Worldwide and a Bachelor's in Business from Florida State University. She founded PodToBook.ai after experiencing firsthand the challenge of turning podcast content into a book.

Based in Florida, she invites service-based entrepreneurs ready to step into their leadership to connect via her company website.

Website: sheilaslick.com
LinkedIn: linkedin.com/in/sheilaslick
Instagram: instagram.com/sheilaslick

Chris O'Byrne

Chris O'Byrne is Founder and CEO of *Jetlaunch Publishing*, an international publishing firm that has empowered thousands of authors and produced over 16,000 books.

With a strong background in systems, strategy, and publishing operations (including leadership roles with Strategic Advisor Board), Chris integrates his know-how in revenue growth, author branding, and business systems to help professionals amplify their voice, build their platform, and scale their impact.

Deeply committed to supporting mission-driven authors and entrepreneurs, he invites you to learn how to attract more clients and generate leads at bookwealthsystem.com and connect via LinkedIn at www.linkedin.com/in/chrisobyrne.

Mariette Snyman

Mariette Snyman is an award-winning South African journalist and the host of the weekly podcast series *Calm, Clear & Helpful*, where she explores wellness, life transitions and practical growth with expert guests.

With more than 30 years of experience interviewing people about life's triumphs and challenges—from parenting and divorce to reinvention and grief—Mariette brings curiosity, compassion and clarity to every conversation.

Based in Johannesburg, she invites wellness professionals, individuals bringing about transformation, and fellow podcasters who are a good fit to listen to Calm, Clear & Helpful and connect with her through her website.

Mariette delights in offering listeners and readers a thoughtful journey of discovering more joy, meaning and self-understanding. Learn more at www.mariettesnyman.co.za

Kevin L. Beers

Kevin Beers is a seasoned software engineer, financial services professional, and marketing consultant turned entrepreneurial mentor. Kevin began his career repairing mainframe hardware and transitioned into software engineering in Richmond, Virginia. Since 2012, he has been educating individuals on how money works and guiding entrepreneurs toward financial literacy. As one of the co-hosts of the podcast Survival Mode, he helps business owners from idea to launch, combining practical financial, technical, and marketing insight.

Website/Contact: www.survivalmode.live | kevin.beers@ bfenterprisesva.com

Bertram G. Robinson Sr

Bert Robinson brings over 30 years of experience in leadership development, human resources, and coaching teams across business and non-profit sectors. As a co-host of Survival Mode, Bert leverages his background in strength-based leadership, organizational clarity, and team culture to help entrepreneurs build sustainable business foundations.

Michael A. Grant Jr

Michael Grant Jr. has been a business consultant for over 15 years, and he has been recognized and was awarded by Inc. magazine for establishing one of the Fastest Growing Companies In America in 2015. He now co-hosts Survival Mode, guiding emerging entrepreneurs through strategy, model-building, and launch execution, focusing on turning side hustles and ideas into structured, scalable ventures.

Website / Contact: www.SurvivalMode.live | mGrant@ MichaelGrantCo.com

Gayle Turner

Gayle Turner is President of *The Storytellers Channel, Inc.*, where he guides individuals in bringing their lived experiences to life through crafted, intentional storytelling. His work blends performance, presence, and personal reflection, helping people find their voice and share it with confidence and clarity.

Gayle continues to teach that stories are not entertainment — they are how we understand who we are, what we value, who we serve, and the impact we create together.

If your values are the North Star that guides your leadership stories, the first step is charting them. Visit StorytellersChannel. com, complete the Culture Compass, and then book a conversation with Gayle to explore how your values can strengthen your organization's performance.

Shelli Jost Brady

Shelli Jost Brady is a co-curator and teaching artist with The Storytellers Channel, where she helps leaders and organizations use the power of story to spark connection, inspire action, and build cultures that last. Shelli uses stories as a strategic tool to navigate change, shape identity, and strengthen trust in corporate and community settings.

She believes that stories plant the seeds of belonging, and that when we tell our stories, we cultivate strong communities.

Because values are meant to guide your leadership, clarity is non-negotiable. Start with the Culture Compass at storytellerschannel.com. Once you've completed it, schedule a conversation with Shelli to discuss how values-aligned leadership strengthens culture and drives higher organizational performance.

Raj Kapur

Raj Kapur is the founder and CEO of Options Ahead, Inc., a wealth mindset expert and former nonprofit CFO with more than 30 years of experience transforming individuals and organizations. Arriving in the US with only $20 and a dream, he went on to build multiple successful businesses and develop the Guidance to Wealth™ framework, helping clients overcome limiting beliefs and achieve financial independence. Raj is a Maxwell Leadership certified coach, DiSC consultant, neuroencoding specialist, and trusted advisor to coaches, consultants, and nonprofit leaders seeking clarity, confidence, and sustainable impact. He resides in Alexandria, VA, and welcomes connection through his website or LinkedIn.

Website: optionsahead.com
LinkedIn: linkedin.com/in/rajkapurmba

Wayne Carroll

Wayne Carroll (J.D., Registered Patent Attorney) is the founder and CEO of *Inspired Idea Solutions® Law Firm*, a firm focused on intellectual property strategy for visionary entre-preneurs, company owners, and CEOs. With over 20 years of IP experience and admission to the US Patent and Trademark Office and the Arizona State Bar, Wayne helps innovators turn their ideas and brands into protected, profitable business assets through strategic use of patents, trademarks, trade secrets, and copyrights.

As host of the syndicated radio show *Leveraging INSPIRATION™* – The Inspired Patent Radio Show, Wayne brings legal clarity to modern creators, explaining complex IP concepts in plain English while empowering leaders to see intellectual property as a strategic growth lever. www.LeveragingINSPIRATION.com Wayne invites service-driven professionals, product creators, and brand builders to explore how protecting their ideas and brands can unlock new opportunities for growth, collaboration, and long-term success. He lives in Arizona and enjoys pickleball and spending time with his children and grandchildren.

Connect with Wayne linkedin.com/in/waynecarroll
Learn more at www.inspiredideasolutions.com.

ACKNOWLEDGMENTS

[*JAMES*] First, I give thanks to God. Every opportunity, every connection, and every assignment in my life flows from His grace. This book is a reminder that when we walk in obedience and purpose, God uses our gifts to encourage, uplift, and equip others. I am grateful for His guidance, provision, and clarity that He continues to give me in the work I am called to do.

To my wife, Melba! Thank you for your love, strength, and unwavering support. You are the foundation that keeps me steady and the partner who helps me grow into the man and leader God is shaping me to be. I couldn't do this without you.

To our sons, James III and Nathaniel, you inspire me every day. Your curiosity, courage, and character remind me why my work matters. My hope is that you always lead with integrity, walk confidently in your calling, and know that your dad is cheering you on.

To every leader who contributed to this book, thank you for showing up with honesty, vulnerability, and intention. Your willingness to share your experiences is an act of leadership that will impact people far beyond these pages.

To the communities that surround and strengthen this work, the clients I coach, the teams I advise, and the leaders I support, thank you for trusting me with your growth and your goals. You challenge me to refine my message, elevate my thinking, and show up with excellence.

To the members of the **Podcast Profit Mastermind,** thank you for your openness, your collaboration, and your willingness

143

to grow as entrepreneurs and communicators. The community we've created is a powerful example of what happens when people come together with purpose.

And finally, to **Donna Kunde**, thank you for your dedication, partnership, and shared commitment to helping others use their message to create real impact. Working alongside you has been a blessing, and this book reflects the strength of what we've built together.

The Coach in Your Corner
Dr. James Bryant

[*DONNA*] To everyone who has ever said yes to sharing your voice, thank you.

This book exists because you were willing to speak, to serve, and to keep showing up even when it felt hard. Every conversation, every story, and every moment of courage has shaped something none of us could have built alone.

To my friends and family, thank you for your patience through the long days, late nights, and crazy dreams!

To my colleagues and clients, thank you for trusting this work and walking beside me.

To Ben, thank you for saying yes to the radio show that started it all.

To James, thank you for your friendship and for building the Podcast Profit System with me.

And to those cheering quietly from the sidelines, your support has meant more than you know.

Here's to all of us who keep using our voices to create a greater global impact.

With gratitude,
Donna

www.ingramcontent.com/pod-product-compliance
Lightning Source LLC
Chambersburg PA
CBHW020155200326
41521CB00006B/382